The Latest Multicooker Cookbook

300+ quick and easy recipes for every occasion

Ursula B. Mendez

©copyright 2024 all right reserved

TABLE OF CONTENT

INTRODUCTION

Welcome to "The Latest Multicooker Cookbook," the definitive multi-cooking resource. The multicooker has become an indispensable domestic appliance in the context of contemporary life, revolutionizing the way we consume food and simplifying the process of cooking. This cookbook is designed to help you optimize this adaptable appliance, regardless of whether you are a culinary enthusiast seeking to experiment with new techniques, a home chef seeking to simplify your routine, or a busy professional.

By incorporating multiple appliances, multicookers have revolutionized the way we cook at home. These devices are capable of sautéing, steaming, slow cooking, pressure cooking, and generating yogurt with the touch of a button. This adaptability expands the range of culinary options and saves time and space. Consider the possibility of preparing a delectable stew in under an hour, creating a stunning cheesecake without the use of an oven, or preparing a nutritious breakfast while you are asleep. A multicooker enables the execution of all of these tasks and more.

Several recipes that are specific to multicookers are included in this compendium. From cosmopolitan delights and comfort cuisine to healthy, innovative dishes and sumptuous sweets, there is something for everyone. Each recipe optimizes the multicooker's capabilities to prepare effortless, delectable meals.

Prior to commencing the recipes, familiarize yourself with the operation of your multicooker. Safety standards, maintenance advice, and essential recommendations are provided to guarantee optimal outcomes. By comprehending the operation of your multicooker, you can modify your preferred recipes and experiment with new ones.

In addition to their convenience, multicookers offer numerous benefits. Ovens and stovetops consume more electricity than energy-efficient multicookers. Additionally, nutrients are preserved as a result of the precise temperature control and expedited culinary process. You will spend less time cooking and more time dining as a result of the reduced number of pots and pans that need to be cleaned.

You are not alone in your pursuit of multi-cooking. To exchange recipes, troubleshoot issues, and share advice, visit the growing online multicooker community. There are an infinite number of applications for this remarkable cooking utensil.

This cookbook is intended to motivate you to prepare meals that are both innovative and daring. "The Most Recent Multicooker Cookbook" will provide you with the necessary information to prepare meals for special occasions, weeknight dinners, and meal planning. Have a wonderful culinary experience!

USING YOUR MULTICOOKER

It is effortless to initiate use of your multicooker; however, comprehending its diverse capabilities and configurations will enable you to optimize this potent appliance. The following is a concise summary of the primary features that are present in the majority of multicookers:

Functions and Settings

Pressure Cook: This function is ideal for dishes that typically require a lengthy cooking time, such as stews, legumes, and difficult portions of meat, as it employs high pressure to prepare food rapidly.

Slow Cook: The slow cook function is the perfect choice for preparing soups, stews, and braised dishes. By setting the multicooker to low and allowing it to percolate for several hours, the ingredients are tenderized, and flavors are infused.

Sauté/Brown: The sauté function in the multicooker can be employed to directly roast meats or sauté vegetables prior to pressure or slow cooking. This eliminates the necessity for additional plates and utensils.

Steam: The steam function is an excellent choice for cooking vegetables, seafood, and even dumplings, as it helps to retain the nutrients & flavors.

Rice Cooker: Numerous multicookers are equipped with a rice cooking preset, which guarantees that the rice is prepared to perfection every time, regardless of whether it is white, brown, or risotto style.

Yogurt Maker: Certain models are equipped with a yogurt-making feature that enables you to ferment your yogurt at home, thereby allowing you to personalize it to your liking.

Basic Operation

Preparation: To begin, prepare the ingredients in accordance with the recipe. Cut vegetables, marinate meats, and measure liquids and seasonings.

Preheat (if necessary): Before adding ingredients, certain recipes may necessitate that the multicooker be preheated using the sauté function.

Add Ingredients: Add the ingredients to the multicooker in accordance with the recipe instructions. Ensure that the utmost fill line indicated inside the vessel is not exceeded.

Select Function and Time: Select the appropriate culinary function and configure the timer in accordance with the recipe. Ensure that the vent is properly configured for pressure cooking and that the lid is securely fastened.

Start Cooking: Press the "start" icon. The multicooker will require some time to establish pressure before the timer commences to tally down during pressure cooking.

Release Pressure: You will need to relieve the pressure after the pressure boiling process is complete. This can be accomplished either rapidly (fast release) or gradually (natural release), contingent upon the recipe.

Serve and Enjoy: Open the lid with care, agitate if necessary, and serve your delectable domestic meal after the cooking process has concluded.

TIPS FOR PERFECT COOKING

Read the Manual: Become acquainted with the user manual for your multicooker model. Comprehending its capabilities will facilitate its utilization.

Layering Ingredients: Denser, more durable ingredients should be placed at the bottom of the pressure cooker, while lighter, more delicate ingredients should be placed on top. This guarantees uniform preparation.

Liquid Matters: Ensure that an adequate amount of liquid is used when preparing under pressure. In order to produce vapor and develop pressure, the multicooker necessitates liquid. The minimum quantity necessary is typically specified in the majority of recipes.

Avoid Overfilling: Make sure that your multicooker is never more than two-thirds filled when you are pressure cooking. To prevent the pressure release valve from becoming obstructed, load foods that expand (such as grains or legumes) only midway.

Natural vs. Quick Release: Understand when to employ natural release and when to use rapid release. Soups and stews are more suitable for natural release, while vegetables and seafood are better suited for rapid release.

Experiment with Sautéing: If your recipe specifies sautéing, refrain from skipping it. Sautéing contributes to the development of a rich, succulent flavor and adds depth of flavor.

Adjust Seasonings: It is advisable to adjust seasonings after cooking, as pressure cooking can occasionally enhance flavors. Taste your dish and adjust the seasonings with additional salt, pepper, or spices as necessary.

Use the Right Tools: To prevent the interior saucepan of your multicooker from being scratched, utilize wooden or silicone implements.

Clean Regularly: It is imperative to conduct routine maintenance on your multicooker. To guarantee hygiene and longevity, it is imperative to clean the interior vessel, lid, and securing ring after each use.

1. BBQ RIBS

Total Time: 30 minute | Prep Time: 10 minutes

Ingredients:

1 lb pork ribs, cut into individual pieces

1 cup water

2 cloves garlic, minced

1 cup BBQ sauce

1 onion, sliced

Salt and pepper to taste

Directions:

(1) Use salt and pepper to season the ribs. *(2)* In the rice cooker, put the ribs. Add the minced garlic & the chopped onion. *(3)* Over the ribs, drizzle the BBQ sauce and water. *(4)* Close the lid once the rice cooker is on the "Cook" setting. Simmer for twenty minutes . *(5)* After the cooking cycle is over, feel for softness in the ribs. Cook for a further five to ten minutes, if necessary. *(6)* With additional BBQ sauce on the side, serve the ribs hot.

2. CHICKEN RADIATOR

Total Time: 30 minutes | Prep Time: 10 minutes

Ingredients:

2 boneless, skinless chicken breasts

1 1/2 cups chicken broth

1/2 cup grated Parmesan cheese

1 clove garlic, minced

Salt and pepper to taste

1 cup radiatori pasta

1 cup marinara sauce

1 tbsp olive oil

1 tsp dried oregano

Directions:

(1) The rice cooker's "Cook" option is the best way to heat olive oil. *(2)* Before adding the chicken, heat for about 5 minutes or until just beginning to brown. *(3)* Cook for a further minute after adding the minced garlic. *(4)* After adding the radiator pasta, pour in the chicken broth. Mix thoroughly. *(5)* After 10 minutes of cooking, cover and let cook. *(6)* Remove the cover and stir in the marinara sauce, dry oregano, and pepper. *(7)* Ten more minutes of cooking time, covered, should be enough to soften the pasta. *(8)* Garnish with grated Parmesan just before serving.

3. REUBEN SANDWICH

Total Time: 30 minutes | Prep Time: 10 minutes

Ingredients:

1/2 lb corned beef, thinly sliced

1 cup sauerkraut, drained

4 slices Swiss cheese

4 slices rye bread

1/4 cup Russian dressing

2 tbsp butter

Directions:

(1) Butter one side of each rye bread piece. *(2)* Butter one side of each bread piece and place the butter in the rice cooker. *(3)* Pile on the sauerkraut, Swiss cheese, corned meat, and Russian dressing. *(4)* Arrange the remaining bread pieces on top, with the butter sides facing upward. *(5)* Once the bread has become a golden-brown color, cover and cook for another five to seven minutes using the

"Cook" option. *(6)* To get melted cheese and crisp bread, gently flip the sandwiches and cook for 7 to 10 minutes. *(7)* Quickly plate the sandwiches.

4. PASTA SALAD

Total Time: 30 minutes | Prep Time: 10 minutes

Ingredients:

2 cups rotini pasta
1 cup cherry tomatoes, halved
1/4 cup red onion, finely chopped
1/4 cup feta cheese, crumbled
Salt and pepper to taste

1 1/2 cups water
1/2 cup cucumber, diced
1/4 cup black olives, sliced
1/4 cup Italian dressing

Directions:

(1) To the rice cooker, add the rotini pasta and water. Ten minutes of cooking time should be enough to soften the spaghetti, so be sure to cover the pot. *(2)* After draining the pasta, set it aside to cool for a little. *(3)* All of the cooked pasta, cucumber, cherry tomatoes, red onion, black olives, and feta cheese should be mixed together in a big basin. *(4)* Toss the macaroni salad with the Italian dressing until well-coated. *(5)* Taste & add salt & pepper as needed. *(6)* The pasta salad may be served cold or at room temperature.

5. SAGANAKI

Total Time: 30 minutes | Prep Time: 10 minutes

Ingredients:

1/2 lb kefalotyri or kasseri cheese
1/4 cup olive oil

1/2 cup all-purpose flour
1 lemon, cut into wedges

Fresh parsley, chopped (for garnish)

Directions:

(1) Toss the cheese slices in flour so they're coated all over. *(2)* The rice cooker's "Cook" option is the best way to heat olive oil. *(3)* Fry the breaded cheese slices for three to four minutes in the heated oil or until they become a golden brown color. *(4)* After the cheese has cooked in the rice cooker, carefully transfer it to a serving platter. *(5)* Top the melted cheese with a squeeze of fresh lemon juice. *(6)* Serve hot with sliced lemons and a sprinkle of minced parsley for garnish.

6. CHICKEN FLORENTINE

Total time: 30 minutes | Prep Time: 10 minutes

Ingredients:

1 cup of uncooked white rice
1/2 cup heavy cream

2 cups fresh spinach, chopped
1 small onion, diced

1 1/2 cups of chicken broth
1 lb boneless, skinless chicken breast, cubed
1/2 cup grated Parmesan cheese
2 cloves garlic, minced
2 tbsp olive oil
Salt and pepper to taste

Directions:

(1) Toss in the rice, olive oil, chicken cubes, onion dice, and garlic powder before starting the rice cooker. While the onions become transparent and the chicken browns, sauté

them. *(2)* Coat the uncooked rice with oil by adding it and stirring well. *(3)* After seasoning with salt and pepper, pour in the heavy cream and chicken broth. *(4)* Put the rice cooker on the "Cook" setting and cover it. Cook for around fifteen to twenty minutes . *(5)* After the rice cooker reaches the "Warm" setting, remove the lid & mix in the spinach & Parmesan cheese that has been diced. *(6)* To melt the cheese & wilt the spinach, cover and simmer on "Warm" for 5 more minutes. *(7)* Hot is best.

7. CHICKEN PACCHERI

Total time: 30 minutes | Prep Time: 10 minutes

Ingredients:

8 oz Paccheri pasta (or rigatoni)	1 lb boneless, skinless chicken thighs, cubed
2 cups marinara sauce	1 cup chicken broth
1/2 cup grated Parmesan cheese	1/2 cup heavy cream
1 small onion, diced	2 cloves garlic, minced
2 tbsp olive oil	Salt and pepper to taste

Directions:

(1) Toss in the rice, olive oil, chicken cubes, onion dice, and garlic powder before starting the rice cooker. While the onions become transparent and the chicken browns, sauté them. *(2)* Mix in the uncooked Paccheri pasta well. *(3)* After adding the chicken stock, heavy cream, and marinara sauce, season with pepper and salt. *(4)* Put the rice cooker on the "Cook" setting and cover it. Cook, stirring periodically, for 20 to 25 minutes . *(5)* Toss in the grated Parmesan cheese after the pasta reaches the doneness you choose. *(6)* The sauce will thicken if you let it rest for a few minutes. *(7)* Hot is best.

8. CHICKEN CAVATAPPI

Total time: 30 minutes | Prep Time: 10 minutes

Ingredients:

8 oz Cavatappi pasta	1 lb boneless, skinless chicken breast, sliced
2 cups chicken broth	1 cup heavy cream
1/2 cup grated Parmesan cheese	1 cup cherry tomatoes, halved
1 small onion, diced	2 cloves garlic, minced
2 tbsp olive oil	Salt and pepper to taste
Fresh basil for garnish	

Directions:

(1) Toss in the olive oil, chicken, onion, and garlic before starting the rice cooker. While the onions become transparent and the chicken browns, sauté them. *(2)* Include the raw Cavatappi pasta and toss to combine. *(3)* After seasoning with salt and pepper, pour in the heavy cream and chicken broth. *(4)* Put the rice cooker on the "Cook" setting and cover it. Cook, stirring periodically, for 20 to 25 minutes . *(5)* After the pasta reaches the doneness you choose, combine it with the cherry tomatoes and grated Parmesan. *(6)* The sauce will thicken if you let it rest for a few minutes. *(7)* Prior to serving, top with fresh basil.

9. PAD THAI

Total time: 30 minutes | Prep Time: 10 minutes

Ingredients:

8 oz rice noodles	1 lb boneless, skinless chicken breast

2 eggs, lightly beaten
1/2 cup crushed peanuts
2 cloves garlic, minced
2 tbsp fish sauce
1 tbsp tamarind paste
2 tbsp vegetable oil

1 cup bean sprouts
3 green onions, chopped
3 tbsp soy sauce
2 tbsp brown sugar
1 lime, cut into wedges

Directions:

(1) Once the rice cooker is turned on, add the sliced chicken, minced garlic, and vegetable oil. Cook the poultry until the interior is no longer raw in a skillet. *(2)* Transfer the chicken to a separate area and pour the beaten eggs into it. Whip the eggs in a skillet until they're done. *(3)* Toss in the ramen, fish sauce, brown sugar, tamarind paste, soy sauce, and rice noodles. Make sure to mix everything well. *(4)* Put the rice cooker on the "Cook" setting and cover it. Turn the heat down to low and simmer, stirring periodically, for 10 to 15 minutes . *(5)* Incorporate the bean sprouts and green onions into the cooked noodles after they reach a tenderness. *(6)* Garnish with crushed peanuts & serve hot with lime wedges on the side.

10.   VEGGIE WRAPS

Total time: 30 minutes | Prep Time: 10 minutes

Ingredients:

1 cup uncooked brown rice
1 cup black beans, drained and rinsed
1 bell pepper, diced
2 cloves garlic, minced
1 tsp chili powder
8 large flour tortillas
1/2 cup salsa
1/2 cup shredded cheddar cheese

1 1/2 cups vegetable broth
1 cup corn kernels
1 small red onion, diced
1 tsp cumin powder
Salt and pepper to taste
1 cup shredded Lettuce
1/2 cup sour cream

Directions:

(1) Toss in the rice cooker with the following ingredients: black beans, corn, brown rice, vegetable broth, bell pepper, red onion, cumin, chili powder, and chopped garlic. Make sure to mix everything well. *(2)* Put the rice cooker on the "Cook" setting and cover it. After twenty to twenty-five minutes , the rice should be soft, and the liquid should have evaporated. *(3)* Taste & add salt & pepper as needed. *(4)* Use a microwave or a skillet to warm the flour tortillas. *(5)* Arrange a spoonful of rice mixture in the middle of each tortilla. Next, garnish with shredded cheddar cheese, salsa, sour cream, and shredded Lettuce. *(6)* Wrap the tortillas and take them out to the table right away.

11.   CHICKEN VESUVIO

Total Time: 30 minutes | Prep Time: 10 minutes

Ingredients:

2 boneless, skinless chicken breasts
1 teaspoon garlic powder
1 teaspoon dried thyme
1/2 teaspoon black pepper

1 tablespoon olive oil
1 teaspoon dried oregano
1/2 teaspoon salt
1 cup chicken broth

1/2 cup white wine
1 cup frozen peas
1/4 cup fresh parsley, chopped

1 cup small red potatoes, quartered
2 cloves garlic, minced

Directions:

(1) Prepare the Chicken: Sprinkle salt, pepper, oregano, and garlic powder on the chicken breasts. **(2)** Sauté the Chicken: Use the "Sauté" setting on the rice cooker, add a little olive oil, and cook the chicken breasts for three to four minutes on each side. **(3)** Add Broth and Wine: Add the white wine and chicken broth, followed by the chopped garlic and quartered potatoes. **(4)** Cook: Once the rice cooker is in "Cook" mode, close the lid. Simmer for fifteen minutes. **(5)** Add Peas: Gently mix in the frozen peas after opening the cover. Once the chicken is well cooked and the potatoes are soft, cover the pan and continue cooking for an additional five minutes. **(6)** Serve: Sprinkle some chopped parsley over top and serve warm.

12.   CAESAR SALAD

Total Time: 15 minutes | Prep Time: 10 minutes

Ingredients:

1 head of romaine lettuce, chopped	1/2 cup grated Parmesan cheese
1 cup croutons	1/4 cup Caesar dressing
1/2 lemon, juiced	2 anchovy fillets, minced (optional)
Freshly ground black pepper	

Directions:

(1) Get the Lettuce Ready: In a large mixing bowl, wash and cut the romaine lettuce. **(2)** To make the dressing, mix the Caesar dressing, lemon juice, and oregano (if using) in a small bowl. Thoroughly combine. **(3)** Toss the Lettuce with the dressing until it is equally coated. Set aside. **(4)** Top it off: Crumbled Parmesan and croutons should be added. Return to the toss phase. **(5)** Place the order: Before serving, sprinkle with freshly ground black pepper.

13.   GIGANTES PLAKI

Total Time: 30 minutes | Prep Time: 10 minutes

Ingredients:

1 cup dried giant beans (soaked overnight)	2 tablespoons olive oil
1 onion, finely chopped	2 cloves garlic, minced
1 can (14 oz) diced tomatoes	1 tablespoon tomato paste
1 teaspoon dried oregano	1 teaspoon dried dill
1 teaspoon salt	1/2 teaspoon black pepper
1/4 cup fresh parsley, chopped	

Directions:

(1) Before you start, make sure the soaked beans are drained and rinsed. **(2)** Add olive oil to the rice cooker & sauté the chopped onion & minced garlic until they become translucent. Then, turn the rice cooker to the "Sauté" setting. **(3)** Season with Salt and Pepper, then & Tomato Paste, Diced Tomatoes, Oregano, Dill, and Tomato Juice. Mix thoroughly. **(4)** To cook the beans, place them in a rice cooker with enough water to cover them and stir to mix. Place the rice cooker cover back on and turn it to the "Cook" setting. **(5)** To cook, cover and simmer for 20 minutes , or until beans are soft and sauce is thick. **(6)** Warm it with some crusty toast and top it with chopped parsley.

14. TZATZIKI

Total Time: 15 minutes | Prep Time: 10 minutes

Ingredients:

1 cup Greek yogurt
2 cloves garlic, minced
1 tablespoon lemon juice
1/2 teaspoon salt

1 cucumber, grated
1 tablespoon olive oil
1 tablespoon fresh dill, chopped
1/4 teaspoon black pepper

Directions:

(1) Get the Cucumber Ready: Grate the cucumber and use paper towels or cheesecloth to press out any extra water. *(2)* Mix What you need: To make the dressing, put the grated cucumber, greek yogurt, garlic, olive oil, lemon juice, dill, salt, and pepper in a measuring cup. *(3)* Make a Good Mix: Combine all ingredients by mixing them well. *(4)* For best results, let it chill in the fridge for 10 minutes before serving. Use it as a spread for pita or a marinade for grilled meats.

15. CHICKEN KIEV

Total Time: 30 minutes | Prep Time: 15 minutes

Ingredients:

2 boneless, skinless chicken breasts
2 cloves garlic, minced
1 teaspoon lemon juice
1/2 cup all-purpose flour
1 cup breadcrumbs

4 tablespoons butter, softened
1 tablespoon fresh parsley, chopped
Salt and pepper to taste
1 egg, beaten
2 tablespoons olive oil

Directions:

(1) Mix melted butter, minced garlic, chopped parsley, lemon juice, salt, & pepper in a small bowl. Wrap the log in plastic and chill until hard. *(2)* Prepare Chicken: Flatten chicken breasts evenly using a meat mallet. *(3)* Stuff Chicken: Put a little hard butter in the middle of each chicken breast. Toothpicks may secure the edges over the butter as you roll it firmly. *(4)* Coat Chicken: Flour, egg, and breadcrumbs, each packed chicken breast. *(5)* Cook Chicken: Brown chicken breasts on both sides in the rice cooker on "Sauté" with olive oil. Close the lid and choose "Cook". After 20 minutes , the chicken should be thoroughly cooked and golden brown. *(6)* Serve hot, with parsley if preferred, and toothpicks removed.

16. COBB SALAD

Total Time: 30 minutes | Prep Time: 15 minutes

Ingredients:

1 cup quinoa, rinsed
2 cooked chicken breasts, diced
1 avocado, diced
1 cup cherry tomatoes, halved

2 cups water
4 slices bacon, cooked and crumbled
2 hard-boiled eggs, chopped
1/2 cup blue cheese, crumbled

1/2 cup green onions, sliced
1/4 cup ranch dressing (optional)

Salt and pepper to taste

Directions:

(1) Add the quinoa & water to the rice cooker. Turn it on to the "Cook" position. After the quinoa has cooked, give it a little fluff with a

fork and set it aside to cool. *(2)* Chicken, bacon, avocado, eggs, tomatoes, blue cheese, green onions, and cooked quinoa should all be mixed together in a big basin. *(3)* Add a little salt & pepper to taste. *(4)* Toss lightly to blend, and then drizzle with ranch dressing if you want. *(5)* Enjoy right away or store in the fridge for later.

17. VEGGIE BURRITOS

Total Time: 30 minutes | Prep Time: 10 minutes

Ingredients:

1 cup rice	2 cups water
1 can black beans, drained and rinsed	1 cup corn kernels (fresh or frozen)
1 red bell pepper, diced	1 green bell pepper, diced
1/2 cup salsa	1 tsp cumin
1 tsp chili powder	Salt and pepper to taste
4 large tortillas	1 cup shredded cheese
1/2 cup sour cream (optional)	1/2 cup guacamole (optional)

Directions:

(1) Add the rice & water to the rice cooker. Turn it on to the "Cook" position. Employ a utensil to agitate the cooked rice. *(2)* Put the cooked rice, black beans, corn, red and green bell peppers, salsa, cumin, chili powder, salt, and pepper into the rice cooker. Stir in the chopped cilantro. Combine ingredients well and warm until heated. *(3)* Divide the filling among the tortillas. Toss on some guacamole, sour cream, and crumbled cheese if you want. *(4)* Encase the tortillas on heated serving platters.

18. BBQ CHICKEN WRAP

Total Time: 30 minutes | Prep Time: 10 minutes

Ingredients:

2 chicken breasts	1 cup BBQ sauce
4 large tortillas	1 cup shredded Lettuce
1/2 cup shredded cheddar cheese	1/4 cup red onion, thinly sliced
1/4 cup pickles, sliced	

Directions:

(1) Add the BBQ sauce to the rice cooker with the chicken breasts. Turn the dial to the "Cook" position and cook for about 20 minutes or until the chicken is done. *(2)* Shred the cooked chicken with two forks & thoroughly combine it with the barbecue sauce. *(3)* Arrange the BBQ chicken, shredded Lettuce, cheddar cheese, red onion, and pickles on top of each tortilla. *(4)* Garnish with rolled tortillas and enjoy right now.

19. FATTOUSH

Total Time: 30 minutes | Prep Time: 15 minutes

Ingredients:

1 cup bulgur wheat	2 cups water
1 cucumber, diced	2 tomatoes, diced
1 red onion, finely chopped	1/4 cup chopped parsley
1/4 cup chopped mint	1/4 cup olive oil
2 tbsp lemon juice	Salt and pepper to taste
2 pieces pita bread, toasted and broken into pieces	

(1) Fill the rice cooker with water and bulgur wheat. Turn it on to the "Cook" position. After the bulgur has cooked, give it a little fluff with a fork and set it aside to cool. (2) Toss together the mint, cucumber, tomatoes, red onion, and parsley in a large bowl. (3) Rub the olive oil, lemon juice, salt, and pepper into a small bowl by whisking them together. (4) After the bulgur is cooked, add it to the vegetable combination and stir in the dressing. (5) For an additional crunch, toss in the toasted pita pieces just before serving.

20.   CHICKEN FARFALLE

Total Time: 30 minutes | Prep Time: 10 minutes

Ingredients:

2 cups farfalle pasta	2 cups chicken broth
1 cup heavy cream	2 cooked chicken breasts, diced
1 cup frozen peas	1/2 cup grated Parmesan cheese
Salt and pepper to taste	1/4 cup chopped fresh basil

Directions:

(1) In a rice cooker, combine farfalle pasta with chicken broth. After about 15 minutes of cooking on the "Cook" setting, the pasta should be al dente. If there's too much broth, strain it. (2) Combine the chicken, peas, Parmesan cheese, heavy cream, salt, and pepper. Stir in the cooked chicken. (3) Once the ingredients are cooked & the sauce has somewhat thickened, cook for another minute or two. (4) Prior to serving, top with fresh basil.

21.   SPLIT PEA SOUP

Total Time: 30 minutes | Prep Time: 10 minutes

Ingredients:

1 cup split peas	4 cups vegetable broth
1 cup diced carrots	1 cup diced celery
1 cup diced onion	2 cloves garlic, minced
1 bay leaf	1 tsp dried thyme
Salt and pepper to taste	1 tbsp olive oil

Directions:

(1) After adding the olive oil to the rice cooker, set it to the "Cook" option. (2) Toss in the chopped garlic, carrots, onion, and celery when the oil has heated. After 5 minutes of sautéing, the veggies should be tender. (3) Toss in the split peas, veggie stock, bay leaf, and dried thyme. Mix thoroughly. (4) After 20 minutes of cooking, cover the rice cooker. (5) After 20 minutes, make sure the peas are cooked through. If the peas aren't soft enough, give them another 5 minutes in the pan. (6) Taste & add salt & pepper as needed. (7) Garnish with a piece of crusty bread and serve hot if preferred.

22.   BLT SANDWICH

Total Time: 20 minutes | Prep Time: 10 minutes

Ingredients:

4 slices of bread	8 slices of bacon
1 large tomato, sliced	4 leaves of Lettuce
4 tbsp mayonnaise	Salt and pepper to taste

Directions:

(1) Set the rice cooker to cook in the preheated oven. (2) For around seven or eight minutes , or until the bacon is crisp, add the pieces to the rice cooker. While cooking, turn the pan halfway through. (3) Take the bacon out of the pan and set it on paper towels to drain. (4) Use either the rice cooker or a separate toaster to toast the bread pieces until they get a golden brown color. (5) On one side of each piece of bread, spread 1 tablespoon of mayonnaise. (6) On top of two pieces of bread, layer two slices of bacon, slices of tomato, and a lettuce leaf. Taste & add salt & pepper as needed. (7) Spoon the remaining mayonnaise-side-down bread pieces on top. (8) Half the sandwiches and serve right away.

23.   KALAMARI

Total Time: 30 minutes | Prep Time: 10 minutes

Ingredients:

1 lb squid, cleaned & cut into rings	1 cup all-purpose flour
1 tsp salt	1 tsp black pepper
1 tsp paprika	1 cup buttermilk
Lemon wedges for serving	Oil for frying

Directions:

(1) Combine the flour, paprika, pepper, & salt in a mixing basin. (2) After submerging the calamari rings in the buttermilk, generously dredge them with the flour mixture. (3) While the rice cooker is set to "Cook," heat the oil. (4) Frying the squid rings in batches after the oil is heated takes approximately 2-3 minutes on each side or until they are golden brown and crispy. (5) Take it off and set it aside to dry. (6) Serve immediately after adding lemon slices as a garnish.

24.   CHICKEN BOLOGNESE

Total Time: 30 minutes | Prep Time: 10 minutes

Ingredients:

1 lb ground chicken	1 cup diced onion
1 cup diced carrots	1 cup diced celery
2 cloves garlic, minced	1 can diced tomatoes
1/2 cup chicken broth	1 tsp dried oregano
1 tsp dried basil	Salt and pepper to taste
2 tbsp olive oil	8 oz cooked pasta

Directions:

(1) After adding the olive oil to the rice cooker, set it to the "Cook" option. (2) Toss in the chopped garlic, carrots, onion, and celery when the oil has heated. After 5 minutes of sautéing, the veggies should be tender. (3) Brown the ground chicken, stirring occasionally with a spoon, for around 7 to 10 minutes after adding it to the pan. (4) Toss in the chicken stock, oregano, basil, and chopped tomatoes. Mix thoroughly. (5) Cook the rice for 15 minutes with the cover on the rice cooker. (6) Taste & add salt & pepper as needed. (7) Top-cooked spaghetti with Bolognese sauce.

25.   CHICKEN PICCATA

Total Time: 30 minutes | Prep Time: 10 minutes

Ingredients:

2 boneless, skinless chicken breasts,	1/2 cup all-purpose flour

pounded thin

1/4 cup olive oil

1/4 cup lemon juice

2 tbsp butter

Chopped parsley for garnish

1/2 cup chicken broth

1/4 cup capers, drained

Salt and pepper to taste

Directions:

(1) Mix the pepper and salt into the chicken breasts. After dredging, shake off any excess flour. **(2)** After adding the olive oil to the rice cooker, set it to the "Cook" option. **(3)** Cook the chicken breasts for four to five minutes in heated oil or until they get a golden brown color on both sides. Detach and put aside. **(4)** After scraping the bottom of the rice cooker for any browned remains, add the chicken stock, lemon juice, and capers. **(5)** Remove the cover and return the chicken breasts to the rice cooker after ten minutes. **(6)** Once added, melt the butter into the sauce. **(7)** Serve immediately after garnishing with chopped parsley.

26.   PULLED PORK SANDWICHES

Total Time: 30 minutes | Prep Time: 10 minutes

Ingredients:

1 lb pork shoulder, cut into chunks

1/2 cup water

2 cloves garlic, minced

1 cup coleslaw (optional)

1 cup barbecue sauce

1 onion, thinly sliced

4 hamburger buns

Salt and pepper to taste

Directions:

(1) Salt and pepper the pork pieces before preparing them. **(2)** Prepare the rice cooker: Put the onions, garlic, barbecue sauce, water, meat, and rice cooker into the cooker. Mix thoroughly. **(3)** Place the cover back on the rice cooker and turn it to the "Cook" option to start the timer. Once the pork is soft and shreds easily, cook it for 20-25 minutes . **(4)** Mince the Pork: Once the rice cooker is uncovered, shred the pork in the sauce using two forks. **(5)** Fill and Top Sandwiches: For a toasted flavor, toast the hamburger buns. Place the pulled pork on top of the bread and, if desired, garnish with coleslaw. **(6)** Before serving, make sure the food is hot.

27.   RED BEANS AND RICE

Total Time: 30 minutes | Prep Time: 10 minutes

Ingredients:

1 cup long-grain white rice

1/2 onion, finely chopped

2 cloves garlic, minced

1 tsp thyme

2 cups chicken or

1 can (15 oz) red beans, drained and rinsed

1/2 green bell pepper, finely chopped

1 tsp paprika

1/2 tsp cayenne pepper

Salt and pepper to

vegetable broth

2 green onions, sliced (optional)

taste

Directions:

(1) Start by finely chopping the onion and bell pepper. **(2)** Mix all of the ingredients: Pour the broth into the rice cooker along with the red beans, onion, bell pepper, garlic, paprika, thyme, and cayenne pepper. Get everything mixed up by stirring it. **(3)** Place the cover back on the rice cooker and turn it to the "Cook" option to start the timer. After 20 to 25 minutes of cooking, the rice should be soft, and the liquid should have been absorbed. *(4)* Time of Year: Before serving, remove the lid from the rice cooker, add salt and pepper according to your taste, and use a fork to fluff the rice. *(5)* If you'd like, you may garnish it with chopped green onions. *(6)* Spoon: Ladle hot.

28. CHICKEN TIKKA MASALA

Total Time: 30 minutes | Prep Time: 10 minutes

Ingredients:

1 lb boneless, skinless chicken thighs	1 cup plain yogurt
2 tbsp tikka masala spice mix	1 onion, finely chopped
1 can (14 oz) diced tomatoes	1/2 cup heavy cream
2 cloves garlic, minced	1 tsp ginger, minced
2 cups basmati rice	3 cups water
Salt to taste	Fresh cilantro for garnish

Directions:

(1) Mix yogurt and tikka masala spice mix with chicken pieces in a bowl. Make sure it marinates for 5 minutes . *(2)* Prepare vegetables: Mince garlic and ginger, and cut the onion finely. *(3)* Combine ingredients: Put marinated chicken, chopped onion, diced tomatoes, garlic, ginger, and heavy cream in the rice cooker. Mix well. *(4)* Add basmati rice and water. Gently combine everything. *(5)* Set Timer: Close the cover and set the rice cooker to 'Cook.' Chicken and rice should be cooked in 25–30 minutes. *(6)* Season: Open the rice cooker, add salt, and stir gently. *(7)* For garnish, add fresh cilantro. *(8)* Serve hot.

29. BUFFALO CHICKEN DIP

Total Time: 30 minutes | Prep Time: 10 minutes

Ingredients:

1 lb boneless, skinless chicken breast, shredded	1/2 cup hot sauce
1/2 cup ranch dressing	1/2 cup cream cheese, softened
1 cup shredded cheddar cheese	2 green onions, sliced
Tortilla chips or celery sticks for serving	

Directions:

(1) First, get the chicken breasts ready by cooking and shredding them. *(2)* Mix all of the ingredients: When the rice cooker is ready, throw in some shredded chicken, spicy sauce, ranch dressing, cream cheese, and cheddar cheese. Mix thoroughly. *(3)* Place the cover back on the rice cooker and turn it to the "Cook" option to start the timer. Stirring periodically, cook for 20 to 25 minutes or until the cheese melts & the mixture is smooth. *(4)* After you've opened the rice cooker, swirl the dip to garnish. Add sliced green onions as a garnish. *(5)* Toppings: tortilla chips or celery sticks go well with this spicy dish.

30. VEGGIE KEBABS

Total Time: 30 minutes | Prep Time: 10 minutes

Ingredients:

1 zucchini, sliced into rounds	1 bell pepper, cut into chunks

1 red onion, cut into chunks

1/2 cup mushrooms, halved

1 tsp Italian seasoning

1 cup couscous

Wooden skewers, soaked in water for ten minutes

1 cup cherry tomatoes

2 tbsp olive oil

Salt and pepper to taste

1 1/2 cups vegetable broth

Directions:

(1) Gather the Vegetables: Chop the veggies into bite-sized pieces. **(2)** Vegetable Marination: Combine olive oil, Italian seasoning, salt, & pepper in a bowl, & then mix in the veggies. **(3)** Make Veggie Skewers: Put the wet wooden skewers through their paces with the marinated veggies. **(4)** Prepare the rice cooker: After arranging the skewers so they fit in the rice cooker, put them in. After placing the cover on top, turn the rice cooker to the "Cook" option. Just a few minutes in the oven should be enough to soften the veggies. **(5)** Prepare the couscous by adding it to a separate rice cooker or saucepan along with the vegetable broth while the vegetables are boiling. After cooking for 5 minutes, set it to "Sit" to soak up any excess liquid. **(6)** To serve, top the vegetable kebabs with the couscous.

31.   LINGUINE WITH CLAMS

Total time: 30 minutes | Prep Time: 10 minutes

Ingredients:

200g linguine

2 cloves garlic, minced

1/2 cup chicken broth

1/4 teaspoon red pepper flakes

Salt and pepper to taste

1 can (10 oz) clams, drained and liquid reserved

1/4 cup white wine

1/4 cup chopped fresh parsley

2 tablespoons olive oil

Directions:

(1) To make al dente linguine, follow the manufacturer's directions and cook it in a rice cooker. Rinse and reserve. **(2)** Warm the olive oil in the rice cooker and stir in the minced garlic. While cooking, let the aroma develop. **(3)** Add the chicken broth & white wine & mix well. **(4)** Reduce heat to low and stir in the clam juice that you set aside. **(5)** Add the clams, cooked linguine, red pepper flakes, and parsley, and stir to combine. **(6)** Toss in some salt and pepper and stir to combine. **(7)** Quickly serve with more parsley on top, if preferred.

32.   CLAM CHOWDER

Total time: 30 minutes | Prep Time: 10 minutes

Ingredients:

1 can (10 oz) clams, drained and liquid reserved

1 onion, diced

1 carrot, diced

1 cup chicken broth

1 bay leaf

2 potatoes, peeled and diced

2 celery stalks, diced

1 cup milk

2 tablespoons butter

1/4 teaspoon thyme

Salt and pepper to taste

Directions:

(1) Put the butter in the rice cooker and set it to cook. **(2)** Carrot, celery, and onion should be added. Keep cooking until the veggies are tender. **(3)** Toss in the potatoes, chicken stock, and clam juice that have been set aside. *(4)* Combine the bay leaf with the thyme. *(5)* After the potatoes have been cooking for about 15 minutes with the cover on, remove them from the rice cooker. *(6)* After adding the milk, mix in the clams. *(7)* Taste & add salt & pepper as needed. *(8)* Heat thoroughly by cooking for another 5 minutes. *(9)* Top with chopped fresh parsley & serve hot.

33. VEGETABLE STIR FRY

Total time: 30 minutes | Prep Time: 10 minutes

Ingredients:

1 cup broccoli florets	1 red bell pepper, sliced
1 yellow bell pepper, sliced	1 carrot, julienned
1 zucchini, sliced	1/4 cup soy sauce
2 tablespoons sesame oil	2 cloves garlic, minced
1 teaspoon grated ginger	one tablespoon cornstarch combined with two tablespoons water
1 tablespoon sesame seeds	

Directions:

(1) Before starting the rice cooker, drizzle it with sesame oil. *(2)* Cook the ginger and garlic until they release their aroma. *(3)* Toss in all the veggies and make sure they're coated with oil. *(4)* After adding the soy sauce, mix well. *(5)* Ten to fifteen minutes after covering the rice cooker, the veggies should be soft. *(6)* While cooking, whisk in the cornstarch mixture to make a thick sauce. *(7)* Serve right away with a sprinkle of sesame seeds.

34. GRILLED SALMON

Total time: 30 minutes | Prep Time: 10 minutes

Ingredients:

2 salmon fillets	2 tablespoons olive oil
2 cloves garlic, minced	1 lemon, sliced
1 teaspoon dried dill	Salt and pepper to taste

Directions:

(1) To preheat the rice cooker, adjust the dial to the "cook" position. *(2)* Before seasoning the salmon fillets with salt, pepper, garlic, and dill, brush them with olive oil. *(3)* After lining the base of the rice cooker with lemon slices, add the salmon fillets. *(4)* When readily flakes with a utensil, the salmon is done cooking. Cover and simmer for around 15-20 minutes . *(5)* Garnish with more lemon wedges, if preferred, and serve right away.

35. BEEF SATAY

Total time: 30 minutes | Prep Time: 10 minutes

Ingredients:

1 lb beef sirloin, thinly sliced	1/4 cup soy sauce
2 tablespoons peanut butter	1 tablespoon brown sugar
2 cloves garlic, minced	1 teaspoon grated ginger
1 tablespoon lime juice	Wooden skewers soaked in water

Directions:

(1) Mix together peanut butter, brown sugar, soy sauce, ginger, garlic & lime juice in a bowl.

(2) Marinate the beef slices for a minimum of 10 minutes after adding them. (3) Poke holes in the steak and thread it onto the moistened skewers. (4) To preheat the rice cooker, adjust the dial to the "cook" position. (5) Lay the skewers flat in the rice cooker. (6) Cook, covered, for 10 to 15 minutes, tossing once halfway through or until the meat is done. (7) If you like it with rice or dipping sauce, you may serve it with either.

36.   HONEY MUSTARD CHICKEN

Total Time: 30 minutes | Prep Time: 10 minutes

Ingredients:

2 boneless, skinless chicken breasts	1/4 cup honey
1/4 cup Dijon mustard	1 tablespoon olive oil
2 garlic cloves, minced	1 teaspoon dried thyme
Salt and pepper to taste	1 cup chicken broth
1 cup rice	

Directions:

(1) Stir honey, Dijon mustard, olive oil, minced garlic, dried thyme, salt, & pepper in a small bowl to make the sauce. (2) Chicken Seasoning: Add chicken breasts to the rice cooker pot and cover with half the honey mustard sauce. Turn to coat evenly. (3) Rice and Broth: Place rice over chicken breasts and pour chicken broth over them. (4) Cook: Close the rice cooker cover and choose "Cook" or "White Rice." Cook until chicken is done and rice is soft, 25–30 minutes . (5) Serve: Carefully open the cover and let the dish sit for 5 minutes. Before serving, drizzle leftover honey mustard sauce over chicken.

37.   CHICKEN GREMOLATA

Total Time: 30 minutes | Prep Time: 10 minutes

Ingredients:

2 boneless, skinless chicken breasts	1 cup rice
1 cup chicken broth	1 lemon (zest and juice)
2 garlic cloves, minced	1/4 cup fresh parsley, chopped
1 tablespoon olive oil	Salt and pepper to taste

Directions:

(1) Gather the ingredients for the gremolata: olive oil, minced garlic, chopped parsley & lemon zest in a small bowl. Put aside. (2) Embellish the Chicken: Mix the pepper and salt into the chicken breasts. (3) Fill the cooker with ingredients: In the rice cooker, add the chicken breasts. Before placing the chicken in the pan, add the stock and rice. (4) Put the rice cooker on the "Cook" or "White Rice" setting and cover it to cook. After the rice is soft and the chicken is done, give it another 25 to 30 minutes to simmer. (5) Carefully remove the cover and set aside for 5 minutes before serving. Toss the chicken with the gremolata and serve.

38.   PECAN-CRUSTED SALMON

Total Time: 30 minutes | Prep Time: 10 minutes

Ingredients:

2 salmon fillets	1/2 cup pecans, finely chopped
1/4 cup panko breadcrumbs	2 tablespoons Dijon mustard

1 tablespoon honey
1 cup rice
Salt and pepper to taste

1 tablespoon olive oil
1 cup vegetable broth

salmon fillets and press the pecan mixture on top. *(3)* Put Ingredients in the cooker: Put salmon fillets in a rice cooker. Put rice and vegetable broth around the fish. *(4)* Cook: Close the rice cooker cover and choose "Cook" or "White Rice." After 20–25 minutes , the fish and rice should be soft. *(5)* Serve: Open the cover gently & let the dish sit for 5 minutes before serving.

(1) Prepare Crust: Mix chopped pecans, panko breadcrumbs, salt, and pepper in a small bowl. *(2)* Coat Salmon: Mix Dijon mustard and honey in another dish. Brush this mixture on the

39.   CAJUN SHRIMP AND GRITS

Total Time: 30 minutes | Prep Time: 10 minutes

Ingredients:

1 pound shrimp, peeled and deveined
1 cup chicken broth
1/4 cup heavy cream

2 tablespoons butter

1/4 cup cheddar cheese, shredded

1 cup quick-cooking grits
1 cup water
1 tablespoon Cajun seasoning
2 garlic cloves, minced
Salt and pepper to taste

with grits, water, chicken stock, & a little pinch of salt. *(3)* Cook Grits: Close the rice cooker cover and choose "Cook" or "White Rice." Cook grits for 20 minutes , stirring periodically, until cooked. *(4)* Finish Grits with Shrimp: Open the cover and add heavy cream, butter, chopped garlic, and grated cheddar cheese to the grits. Top grits with seasoned shrimp. *(5)* Close the lid and simmer the shrimp for 5-7 minutes until pink and cooked through. *(6)* Open the cover gently and let the dish sit for 5 minutes before serving.

Directions:

(1) Toss shrimp with Cajun spice, salt, and pepper. *(2)* To prepare grits, fill the rice cooker

40.   VEGGIE SOUVLAKI

Total Time: 30 minutes | Prep Time: 10 minutes

Ingredients:

1 cup rice
1/2 cup cherry tomatoes, halved
1/4 cup red onion, finely chopped
1/4 cup feta cheese, crumbled
1 tablespoon lemon juice
Salt and pepper to taste

1 cup vegetable broth
1/2 cup cucumber, diced
1/4 cup Kalamata olives, sliced
1 tablespoon olive oil

1 teaspoon dried oregano

Directions:

(1) Toss the chopped veggies with red onion, cherry tomatoes, cucumber, olive oil, salt, pepper, lemon juice, and Kalamata olives in a small bowl. Put aside. *(2)* Prepare the Rice: Toss the rice and veggie stock into the rice cooker pot. *(3)* Put the rice cooker on the "Cook" or "White Rice" setting and cover it to cook. After 25 to 30 minutes of cooking, the rice should be soft. *(4)* Blend and Present: After 5 minutes of resting, gently remove the cover and use a fork to fluff the rice. Stir well after adding the cooked rice to the veggie mixture. *(5)* Before serving, top with crumbled feta cheese.

41. CHICKEN JAMBALAYA

Total Time: 30 minutes | Prep Time: 10 minutes

Ingredients:

2 tablespoons olive oil	1 pound chicken breast, diced
1 andouille sausage, sliced	1 onion, diced
1 green bell pepper, diced	1 celery stalk, diced
2 garlic cloves, minced	1 can (1(4)5 oz) diced tomatoes
1 cup long-grain rice	2 cups chicken broth
1 teaspoon paprika	1 teaspoon dried thyme
1 teaspoon dried oregano	1/2 teaspoon cayenne pepper
Salt and pepper to taste	2 green onions, chopped (for garnish)

Directions:

(1) With the rice cooker set to sauté, heat the olive oil. Brown the sausage and diced chicken in a pan. *(3)* Sauté the garlic, onion, bell pepper, celery, and garlic until cooked through. *(4)* Combine the rice, chicken broth, paprika, thyme, oregano, cayenne pepper, salt, and pepper with the chopped tomatoes. Combine well. *(5)* Put the rice cooker on the "White Rice" setting and cover it. *(6)* Make sure the rice is cooked through and all the liquid has been absorbed. *(7)* Use a fork to fluff, and then top with chopped green onions.

42. PENNE ARRABBIATA

Total Time: 30 minutes | Prep Time: 5 minutes

Ingredients:

2 tablespoons olive oil	4 garlic cloves, minced
1 teaspoon red pepper flakes	1 can crushed tomatoes
1 teaspoon dried oregano	Salt and pepper to taste
1 cup penne pasta	2 cups water
1/4 cup grated Parmesan cheese	Fresh basil leaves for garnish

Directions:

(1) With the rice cooker set to sauté, heat the olive oil. *(2)* Sauté the garlic and red pepper flakes until they release their fragrance. *(3)* Add the oregano, salt, pepper, smashed tomatoes and stir to combine. Fourth, mix the penne pasta with the water, tossing to coat. Fifthly, put the rice cooker on "Pasta" or "Quick Cook" and cover it. *(6)* Simmer until the sauce thickens and the pasta is cooked to al dente. *(7)* Garnish with fresh basil leaves & grated Parmesan cheese.

43. CHICKEN KORMA

Total Time: 30 minutes | Prep Time: 10 minutes

Ingredients:

2 tablespoons vegetable oil	1 onion, diced
2 garlic cloves, minced	1 tablespoon grated ginger
1 pound chicken thighs, diced	1/2 cup plain yogurt
1/4 cup heavy cream	1 can coconut milk
2 tablespoons korma curry paste	1 teaspoon ground coriander
1 teaspoon ground cumin	1 teaspoon turmeric
Salt and pepper to taste	Fresh cilantro, chopped (for garnish)
Cooked rice (for	

serving)

Directions:

(1) Get the rice cooker's sauté function going with some vegetable oil. Add the ginger, garlic, and onion and sauté until the vegetables are tender. Thirdly, brown the diced chicken. *(4)* Combine the yogurt, coconut milk, korma curry paste, kosher salt, pepper, cumin, turmeric, and ground coriander. Stir to combine. *(5)* Secure the cover and use the "Slow Cook" or "White Rice" option on the rice cooker. *(6)* Simmer until the sauce thickens and the chicken is cooked through. *(7)* Top with cooked rice and top with chopped cilantro.

44.   PULLED CHICKEN SANDWICHES

Total Time: 30 minutes | Prep Time: 5 minutes

Ingredients:

2 tablespoons olive oil	1 pound chicken breast
1 onion, sliced	1 cup barbecue sauce
1/2 cup chicken broth	Salt and pepper to taste
4 hamburger buns	Coleslaw (for serving)

Directions:

(1) With the rice cooker set to sauté, heat the olive oil. *(2)* Brown the chicken on both sides after adding the onion and chicken breast. *(3)* Add the chicken broth and barbecue sauce and mix well. *(4)* Lock the lid and choose the "White Rice" option on the rice cooker. *(5)* After the chicken has cooked for a while, it should be soft enough to shred with a fork. *(6)* Mix the chicken and sauce well before shredding. *(7)* Arrange on hamburger buns and accompany with a serving of cabbage.

45.   CHICKEN SAGNE

Total Time: 30 minutes | Prep Time: 10 minutes

Ingredients:

2 tablespoons olive oil	1 pound chicken breast, diced
1 onion, diced	2 garlic cloves, minced
1 cup lasagna noodles broken into pieces	2 cups chicken broth
1 can diced tomatoes	1 teaspoon dried basil
1 teaspoon dried oregano	1/2 teaspoon red pepper flakes
Salt and pepper to taste	1 cup ricotta cheese
1/2 cup shredded mozzarella cheese	Fresh parsley, chopped (for garnish)

Directions:

(1) With the rice cooker set to sauté, heat the olive oil. *(2)* Brown the chopped chicken in the pan. *(3)* Sauté the garlic and onion until they are tender. *(4)* combine the crumbled lasagna noodles with the chicken broth, chopped tomatoes, basil, oregano, salt, pepper, and red pepper flakes. *(5)* put the rice cooker on "Pasta" or "Quick Cook" and cover it. *(6)* Thick the sauce and cook the noodles until they are soft. *(7)* Top with shredded mozzarella cheese, ricotta cheese, and fresh parsley, and serve

46.   CRAWFISH ETOUFFEE

Total Time: 30 minutes | Prep Time: 10 minutes

Ingredients:

1 lb crawfish tails, peeled and cleaned	1 cup white rice
1 cup chicken broth	1 cup diced onions
1 cup diced bell peppers	1 cup diced celery
3 cloves garlic, minced	2 tbsp tomato paste
2 tbsp flour	2 tbsp butter
1 tbsp Cajun seasoning	1 tsp paprika
Salt and pepper to taste	1/4 cup chopped fresh parsley
2 green onions, sliced	Juice of 1 lemon

Directions:

(1) put the butter in the rice cooker and set it to the "Cook" option. *(2)* Saute the celery, bell peppers, onions, and garlic for about 5 minutes or until the vegetables are tender. Three, after two more minutes of simmering, stir in the flour, tomato paste, and garlic. *(4)* Combine the chicken broth, paprika, salt, pepper, Cajun spice, and the other ingredients. Mix thoroughly. *(5)* Mix in the rice and crawfish tails well. *(6)* To cook the rice and thicken the mixture, step 6 covers and heats it for 15 minutes. *(7)* When finished, add the lemon juice, green onions, and parsley and mix to combine. *(8)* Enjoy while hot!

47.   CUBAN SANDWICH

Total Time: 30 minutes | Prep Time: 10 minutes

Ingredients:

4 hoagie rolls or Cuban bread	1/2 lb cooked ham, thinly sliced
1/2 lb roasted pork, thinly sliced	4 slices Swiss cheese
1/2 cup dill pickles, sliced	1/4 cup yellow mustard
2 tbsp butter	

Directions:

(1) Turning the rice cooker to the "Cook" setting to get it hot. *(2)* On the interior of every roll, spread mustard. Put the roasted pork, ham, Swiss cheese, and pickles in an equal layer on top of the three buns. *(4)* Press the sandwiches together and brush the outside of the rolls with the melted butter. *(5)* Depending on the size of the sandwiches, put one or two in the rice cooker and cover it. Toasted bread and melted cheese are the results of 6–7 minutes of cooking time on each side, turning once with a spatula. *(7)* Carry out the same process with the other sandwiches. *(8)* Cut in half and enjoy while still warm.

48.   CHICKEN MARSALA

Total Time: 30 minutes | Prep Time: 10 minutes

Ingredients:

2 boneless, skinless chicken breasts, sliced thinly	1 cup white rice
1 cup chicken broth	1 cup Marsala wine
1 cup mushrooms, sliced	1/2 cup onions, finely chopped
2 cloves garlic, minced	2 tbsp olive oil
2 tbsp flour	1 tbsp butter
Salt and pepper to taste	Fresh parsley for garnish

Directions:

(1) Heat the olive oil and put the rice cooker on the "Cook" setting. *(2)* Brown the chicken

pieces in a skillet over medium heat, adding salt and pepper. This should take around 5 minutes . Take the chicken out and put it aside. *(3)* In the same skillet, melt the butter & sauté the mushrooms and onions for around 5 minutes or until they are soft. *(4)* Cook for a further 2 minutes after adding the flour and garlic. *(5)* Stir in the chicken broth & Marsala wine, then pour in step five. *(6)* Whisk in the rice and then put the chicken back in the cooker. *(7)* Once the rice is done and the sauce has thickened, cover and simmer for another 15 minutes. *(8)* As a garnish, scatter with fresh cilantro before serving.

49.   SPAGHETTI CARBONARA

Total Time: 30 minutes | Prep Time: 10 minutes

Ingredients:

8 oz spaghetti	1/2 cup pancetta or bacon, diced
2 large eggs	1 cup grated Parmesan cheese
3 cloves garlic, minced	1/2 cup heavy cream
Salt and pepper to taste	Fresh parsley, chopped (for garnish)

Directions:

(1) According to the packaging, boil spaghetti in the rice cooker with enough water to cover it. *(2)* Drain and put aside pasta after cooking. *(3)* Put the rice cooker on "Cook" and add pancetta or bacon. Cook for 5 minutes until crispy. *(4)* Add garlic and sauté 2 minutes more. *(5)* Mix eggs, Parmesan, heavy cream, salt, and pepper in a bowl. *(6)* Pour egg mixture over spaghetti in a rice cooker. *(7)* Toss spaghetti to coat evenly and heat for 2-3 minutes until sauce thickens and sticks. *(8)* Add fresh parsley and serve immediately.

50.   CHICKEN MARINARA

Total Time: 30 minutes | Prep Time: 10 minutes

Ingredients:

2 boneless, skinless chicken breasts, sliced thinly	1 cup white rice
1 cup chicken broth	1 cup marinara sauce
1/2 cup onions, finely chopped	2 cloves garlic, minced
1 tbsp olive oil	1 tsp Italian seasoning
Salt and pepper to taste	1/2 cup grated mozzarella cheese
Fresh basil for garnish	

Directions:

(1) Heat the olive oil and put the rice cooker on the "Cook" setting. *(2)* Brown the chicken pieces in a skillet over medium heat, adding salt, pepper, and Italian seasoning. This should take around 5 minutes . Take the chicken out and put it aside. *(3)* Saute the garlic and onions for around three minutes in the same cooker until they are softened. *(4)* Then, while stirring, add the rice, chicken stock, and marinara sauce. Fifthly, stir the chicken before returning it to the stove. Keep the cover on for 15 minutes to cook the rice and thicken the sauce. *(7)* Top with shredded mozzarella and let it melt for two or three minutes. *(8)* Before serving, garnish with fresh basil.

51. CHICKEN FETTUCCINE

Total Time: 30 minutes | Prep Time: 10 minutes

Ingredients:

250g fettuccine pasta

2 cups chicken broth

1/2 cup grated Parmesan cheese

Salt and pepper to taste

1 cup diced chicken breast

1 cup heavy cream

2 cloves garlic, minced

Directions:

(1) Add the chicken broth, heavy cream, garlic, fettuccine, chicken dice, salt, and pepper to the rice cooker. **(2)** Put the rice cooker in "Cook" mode and cover it for 20 minutes . **(3)** After it's done, remove the cover and mix in the grated Parmesan cheese. **(4)** Garnish with parsley if preferred and serve hot.

52. CHICKEN MACARONI

Total Time: 30 minutes | Prep Time: 10 minutes

Ingredients:

2 cups macaroni

1 can diced tomatoes

2 cloves garlic, minced

Salt and pepper to taste

1 cup diced chicken thigh

1 onion, diced

1 teaspoon dried oregano

Directions:

(1) Throw everything into the rice cooker: chopped chicken, diced tomatoes, onion, garlic, dry oregano, macaroni, salt, and pepper. **(2)** Pour in just enough water to submerge the items. **(3)** Put the rice cooker in "Cook" mode and cover it for 20 minutes . **(4)** After that, remove the cover and give it a good stir. **(5)** Warm the dish before serving, and if desired, top with chopped fresh basil.

53. SHAWARMA

Total Time: 30 minutes | Prep Time: 10 minutes

Ingredients:

250g chicken breast, thinly sliced

1 teaspoon ground cumin

1 teaspoon ground turmeric

Salt and pepper to taste

1 tablespoon olive oil

1 teaspoon paprika

1 teaspoon ground coriander

Directions:

(1) The ingredients for the dressing include ground cumin, paprika, turmeric, coriander, olive oil, salt, and pepper. **(2)** Combine the bowl with the thinly cut chicken breast and mix until coated. **(3)** Place the chicken that has been seasoned in the rice cooker. **(4)** Put the rice cooker in "Cook" mode and cover it for 20 minutes . **(5)** When done, remove the cover and add pita bread and tahini sauce for a hot serving.

54. CHICKEN GEMELLI

Total Time: 30 minutes | Prep Time: 10 minutes

Ingredients:

1 cup Gemelli pasta

1 cup diced chicken

thigh

1 cup diced bell peppers

1 cup diced zucchini

1 cup marinara sauce

1/2 cup shredded mozzarella cheese

1 tablespoon olive oil

Directions:

(1) Add the chicken, bell peppers, zucchini, marinara sauce, and olive oil to the rice cooker along with the Gemelli pasta. **(2)** Pour in just enough water to submerge the ingredients. **(3)** Put the rice cooker on "Cook" for 20 minutes with the lid closed. **(4)** The fourth step is to open the cover and top it with shredded mozzarella cheese. **(5)** If desirable, garnish when preparing to serve with fresh basil leaves.

55.   CHICKEN WINGS

Total Time: 30 minutes | Prep Time: 10 minutes

Ingredients:

12 chicken wings

1/2 cup barbecue sauce

2 tablespoons soy sauce

2 tablespoons honey

1 tablespoon olive oil

Salt and pepper to taste

Directions:

(1) Combine the honey, soy sauce, barbecue sauce, olive oil, salt, & pepper in a bowl. **(2)** Toss the chicken wings in the basin until they are covered all over. **(3)** Place the chicken wings in the rice cooker after seasoning. **(4)** Put the rice cooker in "Cook" mode and cover it for 20 minutes . **(5)** When done, remove the cover and serve hot, topping with chopped green onions if desired.

56.   MELITZANOSALATA

Total Time: 25 minutes | Prep Time: 10 minutes

Ingredients:

2 large eggplants

2 cloves garlic, minced

1/4 cup olive oil

2 tablespoons lemon juice

Salt and pepper to taste

2 tablespoons chopped fresh parsley

Directions:

(1) Put all the eggplants into the rice cooker after piercing them with a fork. **(2)** Until tender, which should take about 15 minutes when using the white rice setting. **(3)** Remove cooked eggplants from the pan and set aside to cool. **(4)** Remove the meat & set it aside in a basin. **(5)** Toss the bowl with the minced garlic, olive oil, lemon juice, salt, and pepper. **(6)** Make sure the mixture is smooth by mashing it. **(7)** Add the chopped parsley and mix well. **(8)** Accompany with crackers or pita bread.

57.   CHICKEN GUMBO

Total Time: 30 minutes | Prep Time: 15 minutes

Ingredients:

1 lb chicken breast, diced

1 onion, chopped

1 can diced tomatoes

3 cups chicken broth

1 cup okra, sliced

1 teaspoon Cajun seasoning

1 bell pepper, chopped

2 celery stalks, chopped

Salt and pepper to taste

(1) Throw in some chopped chicken and put the rice cooker on sauté. *(2)* Brown in a skillet, then take out and leave aside. *(3)* Throw in some celery, bell pepper, and onion in the same saucepan. Cook until tender. *(4)* combine the okra, chicken broth, chopped tomatoes, Cajun spice, salt, and pepper. *(5)* Put the chicken back in the saucepan. *(6)* Put the cover on and let it simmer for 15 minutes on the soup setting. *(7)* Toppings: rice and crusty toast. Enjoy hot.

58.   BEEF GYRO

Total Time: 25 minutes | Prep Time: 10 minutes

Ingredients:

1 lb beef sirloin, thinly sliced

2 cloves garlic, minced

2 teaspoons dried oregano

Salt and pepper to taste

1 onion, thinly sliced

2 tablespoons olive oil

1 teaspoon paprika

Pita bread, tzatziki sauce, Lettuce, and tomato for serving

Directions:

(1) Pour the olive oil and put the rice cooker on sauté. *(2)* Brown the cut meat in the pan. *(3)* Grind some garlic and add some chopped onion. Cook until tender. *(4)* Add salt, pepper, paprika, dried oregano, and continue seasoning. *(5)* Put the cover on and cook for 10 minutes with the rice setting. *(6)* Top heated pita bread with beef gyro filling, then top with tzatziki sauce, Lettuce, and tomato.

59.   CHICKEN TROFIE

Total Time: 30 minutes | Prep Time: 15 minutes

Ingredients:

1 lb chicken thighs, diced

1 onion, chopped

1 cup chicken broth

1 cup frozen peas

Salt and pepper to taste

2 cups trofie pasta

2 cloves garlic, minced

1 cup heavy cream

1/4 cup grated Parmesan cheese

Directions:

(1) Throw in some chopped chicken and put the rice cooker on sauté. *(2)* Brown in a skillet, then take out and leave aside. *(3)* Toss in the minced garlic and chopped onion in the same saucepan. Cook until tender. *(4)* Include the trofie pasta, chicken broth, and heavy cream in step four. *(5)* Place the cover on top and cook for 15 minutes with the rice setting. *(6)* Lastly, combine the cooked chicken with the frozen peas. *(7)* Add another 5 minutes of cooking time. *(8)* Garnish with grated Parmesan cheese and serve hot.

60.   FRENCH ONION SOUP

Total Time: 30 minutes | Prep Time: 10 minutes

Ingredients:

4 onions, thinly sliced

4 cups beef broth

2 tablespoons butter

1/2 cup dry white wine (optional)

1 teaspoon Worcestershire sauce

Baguette slices and grated Gruyere cheese

Salt and pepper to taste

for serving

Directions:

(1) Melt the butter and put the rice cooker on sauté mode. (2) Caramelize the onions by adding thinly sliced onions to the pan. (3) Season with salt & pepper and stir in the beef broth, dry white wine (if using), Worcestershire sauce, and oil. (4) Put the cover on and let it cook for 20 minutes in the soup setting. (5) In the meantime, heat up some oven toast. (6) Spoon the soup into oven-safe bowls and garnish with sliced baguette and grated Gruyere. (7) Broil for 7 to 10 minutes or until cheese is melted and bubbling. (8) Serving when still hot.

61.   CHICKEN QUESADILLAS

Total Time: 30 minutes | Prep Time: 15 minutes

Ingredients:

1 cup cooked chicken, shredded	1 cup shredded cheddar cheese
1/2 cup diced onion	1/2 cup diced bell pepper
4 large flour tortillas	1 tablespoon olive oil
1 teaspoon chili powder	1 teaspoon cumin
Salt and pepper to taste	Optional toppings: salsa, sour cream, guacamole

Directions:

(1) The shredded chicken, cheddar cheese, chopped onion, diced bell pepper, chili powder, cumin, salt, & pepper should all be combined in a bowl. (2) Split the chicken mixture in half and put half of it on each tortilla. Set aside two tortillas. (3) To make two quesadillas, fold the tortillas in half and cover the contents. (4) In a big skillet, heat the olive oil over medium heat. (5) To get the quesadillas crispy and golden brown, heat for two or three minutes on each side of the pan. (6) After taking it out of the pan, give it a minute to cool down before cutting it into wedges. (7) Garnish with sour cream, salsa, or guacamole and serve hot.

62.   MALAI KOFTA

Total Time: 30 minutes | Prep Time: 15 minutes

Ingredients:

2 cups mashed potatoes	1 cup paneer (Indian cottage cheese), crumbled
1/4 cup all-purpose flour	2 tablespoons cornstarch
1 teaspoon garam masala	1/2 teaspoon chili powder
Salt to taste	Oil for frying
For the Sauce:	1 onion, chopped
2 tomatoes, chopped	1-inch piece of ginger, minced
2 cloves of garlic, minced	1/2 cup heavy cream
1 teaspoon garam masala	1 teaspoon cumin
Salt to taste	Fresh cilantro for garnish

Directions:

(1) Blend mashed potatoes, crumbled paneer, all-purpose flour, cornstarch, garam masala, chili powder, and salt in a bowl. (2) Make golf ball-sized balls from the mixture. In a deep fryer, heat oil on medium. (3) Carefully drop the kofta balls in the heated oil and cook for 5-6 minutes until golden brown and crispy. Drain excess oil on a paper towel-lined platter. (4) Cook the chopped onion, ginger, and garlic in a little oil in a separate pan until softened. Cook chopped tomatoes until mushy. (5) Mix in heavy cream, garam masala, cumin, and salt. Simmer the sauce for a few minutes to

thicken. *(6)* Add the cooked kofta balls to the sauce gently and coat evenly. *(7)* Add fresh cilantro and serve hot with rice or naan.

63. CHICKEN LINGUINE

Total Time: 30 minutes | Prep Time: 10 minutes

Ingredients:

8 oz linguine pasta	2 chicken breasts, thinly sliced
2 tablespoons olive oil	2 cloves garlic, minced
1 cup cherry tomatoes, halved	1/2 cup fresh spinach leaves
1/4 cup grated Parmesan cheese	Salt and pepper to taste
Fresh basil leaves for garnish	

Directions:

(1) Linguine should be cooked al dente per package directions. Drain and put aside. *(2)* Warm olive oil in a big skillet on medium-high. *(3)* Cook the cut chicken breasts in the skillet for 5-6 minutes each side until golden brown and cooked through. *(4)* Add minced garlic to the pan & sauté for another minute until fragrant. *(5)* Add split cherry tomatoes and fresh spinach leaves and simmer for 2-3 minutes until spinach wilts and tomatoes soften. *(6)* Add cooked linguine to the pan and mix thoroughly. *(7)* Grate Parmesan cheese over linguine and toss again to coat. *(8)* Add salt and pepper to taste. *(9)* Add fresh basil before serving.

64. BEEF SOUVLAKI

Total Time: 30 minutes | Prep Time: 15 minutes

Ingredients:

1 lb beef sirloin, cut into bite-sized pieces	1/4 cup olive oil
2 tablespoons lemon juice	2 cloves garlic, minced
1 teaspoon dried oregano	1/2 teaspoon dried thyme
Salt and pepper to taste	Pita bread for serving
Tzatziki sauce for serving	Sliced tomatoes, onions, and cucumbers for serving

Directions:

(1) Mix olive oil, lemon juice, minced garlic, dried oregano, dried thyme, salt & pepper in a dish to prepare the marinade. *(2)* Place beef sirloin chunks in marinade and coat thoroughly. Marinate for 10 minutes . *(3)* Preheat the rice cooker on "Quick Cook" or similar. *(4)* Put marinated meat on skewers. *(5)* After heating the rice cooker, add the meat skewers and cover. Cook the meat for 8-10 minutes to your preferred doneness. *(6)* Toast or bake pita bread while the meat cooks. *(7)* Serve beef souvlaki with warm pita bread, tzatziki sauce, and sliced tomatoes, onions, and cucumbers.

65. LAMB GYRO

Total Time: 30 minutes | Prep Time: 10 minutes

Ingredients:

1 lb lamb meat, thinly sliced	1 small red onion, thinly sliced
2 cloves garlic, minced	1 tsp dried oregano

1 tsp ground cumin

4 pita bread

Sliced tomatoes

Crumbled feta cheese

Salt and pepper to taste

Tzatziki sauce

Sliced cucumbers

Directions:

(1) Garlic powder, dried oregano, cumin powder, salt, and pepper should be sprinkled over the lamb slices before cooking. *(2)* Season the lamb slices and add them to the rice cooker. *(3)* Before serving, garnish the lamb with chopped red onion. *(4)* Press the "Cook" button on the rice cooker's cover. Finish cooking after 20 minutes . *(5)* Put the pita bread in the oven or microwave to warm while the lamb is cooking. *(6)* Assemble the gyro by stuffing heated pita bread with chopped tomatoes, cucumbers, and cooked lamb. Top with crumbled feta cheese. *(7)* Top the gyro filling with the tzatziki sauce. *(8)* Warm up and savor!

66.   FISH TACOS

Total Time: 30 minutes | Prep Time: 10 minutes

Ingredients:

1 lb white fish fillets

Juice of 1 lime

8 small flour tortillas

Diced tomatoes

Sliced jalapeños

1 tbsp taco seasoning

Salt and pepper to taste

Shredded Lettuce

Sliced avocado

Sour cream or salsa (optional)

Directions:

(1) Sprinkle salt, pepper, lime juice, and taco spice onto the fish fillets. *(2)* In a rice cooker, add the seasoned fish fillets. *(3)* On the lid of the rice cooker, press the "Cook" button. Finish cooking after 20 minutes . *(4)* As the fish cooks, get the taco toppings ready: chopped tomatoes, shredded Lettuce, avocado, and jalapeños. *(5)* After the fish has cooked, use a fork to break it up into pieces. *(6)* Preheat the oven or microwave to reheat the flour tortillas. *(7)* Layer the cooked fish and toppings of your choice into each tortilla to make the fish tacos. *(8)* If preferred, serve hot and garnish with sour cream or salsa.

67.   CHICKEN ARRABBIATA

Total Time: 30 minutes | Prep Time: 10 minutes

Ingredients:

1 lb boneless, skinless chicken breasts, diced

2 cloves garlic, minced

1 tsp crushed red pepper flakes

Cooked pasta of your choice

2 cups marinara sauce

1 tsp dried basil

Salt and pepper to taste

Grated Parmesan cheese (optional)

Directions:

(1) Put the chicken breasts that have been diced into the rice cooker. *(2)* With the salt and pepper, combine the minced garlic with the dried basil and crushed red pepper flakes. *(3)* Coat the chicken with marinara sauce. *(4)* Press the "Cook" button on the rice cooker's cover. Finish cooking after 20 minutes . *(5)* Prepare the pasta as directed on the box while the chicken is in the oven. *(6)* Toss cooked spaghetti with the cooked chicken after it's done cooking. *(7)* If desired, sprinkle with grated Parmesan cheese as a garnish. *(8)* Warm up and savor!

68. GARLIC ROSEMARY CHICKEN

Total Time: 30 minutes | Prep Time: 10 minutes

Ingredients:

1 lb chicken thighs, bone-in

2 tbsp fresh rosemary leaves, chopped

Salt and pepper to taste

4 cloves garlic, minced

2 tbsp olive oil

Lemon wedges for serving

Directions:

(1) Add salt, pepper, olive oil, minced garlic, and chopped rosemary to the chicken thighs for seasoning. *(2)* Before adding the chicken thighs to the rice cooker, season them. *(3)* On the lid of the rice cooker, press the "Cook" button. After 20 minutes , finish cooking. *(4)* Move the cooked chicken to a platter and serve. *(5)* Toss the chicken with the lemon wedges and serve. *(6)* Warm up and savor!

69. THAI GREEN CURRY

Total Time: 30 minutes | Prep Time: 10 minutes

Ingredients:

1 cup jasmine rice

2 tbsp Thai green curry paste

1 cup cooked chicken, sliced

1 tbsp brown sugar

1 can of coconut milk

1 cup mixed vegetables (bell peppers, broccoli, carrots)

2 tbsp fish sauce

Fresh basil leaves for garnish

Directions:

(1) Before adding 2 cups of water to the rice cooker, rinse the jasmine rice. Put it in the oven and close the lid. *(2)* The green curry paste and coconut milk should be mixed well in a bowl. *(3)* After the rice has cooked for a while, throw in the mixed veggies and cut the chicken. *(4)* After you've added the chicken and veggies to the pan, pour the coconut milk mixture. *(5)* Combine the brown sugar and fish sauce. Mix thoroughly. *(6)* Once the veggies are soft, cover & continue cooking for another 10 to 15 minutes . *(7)* Top with fresh basil leaves and serve hot.

70. POTATO LEEK SOUP

Total Time: 30 minutes | Prep Time: 10 minutes

Ingredients:

2 large leeks, chopped

4 cups vegetable broth

Salt and pepper to taste

2 potatoes, peeled and diced

1 cup milk

Fresh chives for garnish

Directions:

(1) Toss diced potatoes and chopped leeks into the rice cooker. *(2)* Add the milk and veggie broth. *(3)* Sprinkle with salt & pepper to taste. *(4)* After 20 minutes of cooking, cover the rice cooker and remove the lid. *(5)* After that, purée the soup using a hand blender. *(6)* Taste and add more spice as needed. *(7)* Top with chopped fresh chives and serve hot.

71. LOBSTER BISQUE

Total Time: 30 minutes | Prep Time: 10 minutes

Ingredients:

2 lobster tails, meat removed and chopped

2 cloves garlic, minced

1 cup heavy cream

Salt and pepper to taste

1 small onion, finely chopped

2 cups seafood stock

2 tbsp tomato paste

Fresh parsley for garnish

Directions:

(1) Saute the minced garlic and diced onion in the rice cooker until they release their wonderful aroma. **(2)** Toss in the diced lobster and keep cooking for another two or three minutes . **(3)** Stir in the tomato paste, heavy cream, and seafood stock. **(4)** Add a little salt & pepper to taste. **(5)** Leave it covered and in the oven for 20 minutes. **(6)** Spoon the bisque into serving dishes when it is ready. **(7)** Prior to serving, top with chopped fresh parsley.

72. CHICKEN ALFREDO

Total Time: 30 minutes | Prep Time: 10 minutes

Ingredients:

1 cup penne pasta

2 cups chicken broth

1 cup grated Parmesan cheese

Salt and pepper to taste

1 cup diced chicken breast

1 cup heavy cream

2 tbsp butter

Fresh parsley for garnish

Directions:

(1) In a rice cooker, simmer the rice with butter, heavy cream, chicken broth, diced chicken breast, & penne pasta. **(2)** Add a little salt & pepper to taste. **(3)** Leave it covered and in the oven for 20 minutes . **(4)** At that point, add the grated Parmesan and mix until smooth and melted. **(5)** Taste and

add more spice as needed. **(6)** Heat and serve with a sprinkle of fresh parsley on top.

73. CHICKEN STROZZAPRETI

Total Time: 30 minutes | Prep Time: 10 minutes

Ingredients:

1 cup Strozzapreti pasta

1 cup cherry tomatoes, halved

2 cloves garlic, minced

Salt and pepper to taste

1 boneless, skinless chicken breast, diced

1/2 cup spinach leaves

2 tablespoons olive oil

Directions:

(1) Get the Strozzapreti pasta ready for the rice cooker by rinsing it under cold water. **(2)** In a rice cooker, combine chopped chicken, cherry tomatoes, spinach, basil, garlic, olive oil, salt, and pepper. **(3)** Put the cover on the rice cooker and cook it for 20 minutes . **(4)** Uncover the lid and stir well before serving it hot.

74.   CHICKEN PUTTANESCA

Total Time: 30 minutes | Prep Time: 10 minutes

Ingredients:

1 cup penne pasta

1/2 cup olives, sliced
1 can (14 oz) diced tomatoes
2 tablespoons olive oil

1 boneless, skinless chicken breast, sliced
1/4 cup capers
2 cloves garlic, minced
Salt and pepper to taste

Directions:

(1) Get the penne pasta ready for the rice cooker by rinsing it under cold water. *(2)* In a rice cooker, combine sliced chicken, capers, olives, tomatoes, garlic, olive oil, salt, and pepper. *(3)* Put the cover on the rice cooker and cook it for 20 minutes . *(4)* Uncover the lid and stir well before serving it hot.

75.   VEGETABLE CURRY

Total Time: 30 minutes | Prep Time: 10 minutes

Ingredients:

1 cup basmati rice

1 onion, chopped
1 can (14 oz) coconut milk
Salt and pepper to taste

1 cup mixed vegetables (carrots, peas, bell peppers)
2 cloves garlic, minced
2 tablespoons curry powder

Directions:

(1) Before adding the basmati rice to the rice cooker, give it a quick rinse in cold water. *(2)* Pour coconut milk, curry powder, chopped onion, minced garlic, salt, pepper, and a variety of veggies into the rice cooker. *(3)* Put the cover on the rice cooker and cook it for 20 minutes . *(4)* Uncover the lid and stir well before serving it hot.

76.   BLACKENED SALMON

Total Time: 30 minutes | Prep Time: 10 minutes

Ingredients:

2 salmon fillets

2 tablespoons olive oil
Salt and pepper to taste

2 tablespoons blackening seasoning
1 lemon, sliced

Directions:

(1) To season the salmon fillets, rub them with blackening spice, olive oil, salt, and pepper. *(2)* in the rice cooker, add the lemon slices and salmon fillets. *(3)* Put the cover on the rice cooker and cook it for 20 minutes . *(4)* When done, remove the cover and serve hot with a side of your choice.

77.   SHRIMP CREOLE

Total Time: 30 minutes | Prep Time: 10 minutes

Ingredients:

1 cup long-grain white rice
1 onion, chopped

1 tablespoon olive oil

1 green bell pepper,

2 cloves garlic, minced
1 teaspoon paprika

chopped
1 can diced tomatoes

1/2 teaspoon dried thyme

1/4 teaspoon cayenne pepper (adjust to taste)

1 pound shrimp, peeled and deveined Cooked rice for serving

Salt and pepper to taste

2 green onions, chopped (for garnish)

Directions:

(1) Make sure the water flows clean after rinsing the rice with cold water. Follow the manufacturer's directions for cooking the rice in the rice cooker. **(2)** Get a big pan going with some medium-high heat and some olive oil while the rice is cooking. Saute the bell peppers & onions for about 5 minutes or until they are tender. **(3)** Cook for an additional minute after adding minced garlic to the pan. **(4)** Toss in the chopped tomatoes, paprika, thyme, cayenne pepper, salt, and pepper. For 10 minutes, let it simmer. **(5)** Cook the shrimp for about 5 minutes, or until they become pink and opaque, in a pan. **(6)** After the rice is done, top it with the shrimp creole and top it off with chopped green onions. Dig it!

78. FALAFEL WRAP

Total Time: 30 minutes | Prep Time: 15 minutes

Ingredients:

1 cup dried chickpeas, soaked overnight

2 cloves garlic

1 teaspoon ground coriander

Salt to taste

2 tablespoons all-purpose flour

4 whole wheat tortillas

Lettuce, tomatoes, cucumbers (optional, for garnish)

1/2 onion, chopped

1 teaspoon ground cumin

1/4 teaspoon cayenne pepper

2 tablespoons chopped fresh parsley

2 tablespoons olive oil

Tzatziki sauce for serving

Directions:

(1) The soaked chickpeas should be drained and rinsed. Blend together the chickpeas, garlic, onion, cumin, cilantro, cayenne pepper, salt, and parsley in a food processor. Crush to a coarse powder. **(2)** Toss in the flour and pulse again until just mixed. **(3)** Form little patties using the ingredients. **(4)** In a skillet set over medium heat, warm the olive oil. Fry the falafel patties for three to four minutes on each side or until they are crispy and golden brown. **(5)** To warm the tortillas, use a pan or microwave. **(6)** Spoon tzatziki sauce over the tortillas, then top with falafel patties and any other toppings you choose. **(7)** Wrap the tortillas in them, slice them in half if you want, and eat them right away. Graze on those falafel wraps!

79. CHICKEN AND RICE CASSEROLE

Total Time: 30 minutes | Prep Time: 10 minutes

Ingredients:

1 cup long-grain white rice

1 pound boneless, skinless chicken breasts, cubed

1 can condensed

1 1/2 cups chicken broth

1 cup frozen mixed vegetables

1/2 cup shredded

cream of chicken soup

Salt and pepper to taste

cheddar cheese

Fresh parsley, chopped (for garnish)

Directions:

(1) After washing the rice in cold water, make sure the water is clear. Following the manufacturer's directions, cook the rice in a rice cooker with chicken stock. *(2)* Preheat the oven to 190°C while the rice is cooking. *(3)* Mix together the cooked rice, chicken cubes, frozen mixed veggies, chicken soup, cheddar cheese, salt, and pepper in a big dish. Add the condensed cream of chicken soup. *(4)* After greasing the baking dish, transfer the mixture and spread it out evenly. *(5)* Cook the chicken and casserole in the oven for 20 to 25 minutes or until the casserole is bubbling and cooked through. *(6)* Add some chopped parsley as a garnish just before serving. Take a bite out of your rice cooker-cooked chicken and rice dish!

80. DOLMADES

Total Time: 30 minutes | Prep Time: 15 minutes

Ingredients:

1 cup white rice	1/4 cup olive oil
1 onion, finely chopped	2 cloves garlic, minced
1/4 cup pine nuts	1/4 cup currants or raisins
1/4 cup chopped fresh dill	1/4 cup chopped fresh mint
Salt and pepper to taste	1 jar (8 ounces) grape leaves, drained and rinsed
Lemon wedges for serving	

Directions:

(2) Rice should be well-cleaned in cold water. Cook and put aside rice according to package directions. *(2)*

Cook olive oil in a skillet on medium. Sauté chopped onions and garlic for 5 minutes until softened. *(3)* Add pine nuts and currants or raisins and simmer for 2-3 minutes. *(4)* Mix cooked rice, chopped dill, and chopped mint after removing from heat. Sprinkle salt and pepper. *(5)* Lay a grape leaf shining side down on a clean surface. Spoon a little rice mixture into the leaf center. *(6)* Fold the leaf's sides over the filling and roll it firmly from bottom to top to make a cylinder. *(7)* Use the leftover grape leaves and rice mixture. *(8)* Offer lemon wedges for squeezing over dolmades. Enjoy this delicious Mediterranean cuisine!

81. VEGGIE CHOPS

Total Time: 30 minutes | Prep Time: 10 minutes

Ingredients:

1 cup mixed vegetables (carrots, peas, corn)	1 cup bread crumbs
½ cup grated cheese	¼ cup chopped cilantro
2 tablespoons olive oil	Salt and pepper to taste

Directions:

(1) Divide the mixed veggies into little pieces and chop them. *(2)* Toss together the chopped veggies, breadcrumbs, cheese, cilantro, olive oil, salt & pepper in a large bowl. *(3)* Ensure that all materials are well combined. *(4)* Shape the ingredients into little patties. *(5)* Twenty minutes , or until they become a golden brown color, throw the patties into the rice cooker. *(6)* Top with your preferred dipping sauce and serve hot.

82.   CHICKEN CARBONARA

Total Time: 30 minutes | Prep Time: 10 minutes

Ingredients:

1 cup diced chicken breast

2 cups cooked spaghetti

2 eggs

Salt and pepper to taste

1/2 cup diced bacon

1/2 cup grated Parmesan cheese

1/2 cup heavy cream

Directions:

(1) Toss the diced chicken breast and bacon in a pan and heat until they become golden. *(2)* Combine the eggs, Parmesan, heavy cream, salt & pepper in a bowl & whisk to combine. *(3)* Toss in the cooked spaghetti with the bacon and chicken in the pan. *(4)* Toss the spaghetti in the egg mixture to coat it well. *(5)* To cook the eggs until they are set, transfer the mixture to a rice cooker & simmer for 10 minutes . *(6)* When served hot, garnish with more Parmesan cheese.

83.   CHICKEN SATAY

Total Time: 30 minutes | Prep Time: 15 minutes

Ingredients:

1 pound chicken breast, cut into strips

2 tablespoons peanut butter

1 tablespoon lime juice

1/2 teaspoon ground ginger

1/4 cup soy sauce

2 tablespoons honey

1 teaspoon minced garlic

Directions:

(1) In a bowl, mix peanut butter, honey, lime juice, minced garlic & crushed ginger to marinate the meat. *(2)* Marinate the chicken strips for a minimum of 10 minutes after adding them to the marinade. *(3)* Skewer the chicken strips that have been marinated. *(4)* After 15 minutes of cooking over high heat, the chicken skewers should be ready. *(5)* Warm and serve with cucumber slices and peanut sauce on the side.

84.   TANDOORI CHICKEN

Total Time: 30 minutes | Prep Time: 10 minutes

Ingredients:

4 chicken thighs, bone-in

2 tablespoons tandoori masala

1 teaspoon minced ginger

Salt to taste

1/2 cup plain yogurt

1 tablespoon lemon juice

1 teaspoon minced garlic

Directions:

(1) Marinade the meat in a bowl with a mixture of yogurt, tandoori masala, lemon juice, chopped garlic, ginger, and salt. *(2)* Cut the chicken thighs into small, shallow slices. *(3)* After tossing & massaging the chicken thighs in the marinade, coat them evenly. *(4)* Ten minutes is the minimum amount of time to marinate the chicken. *(5)* After marinating, cook the chicken thighs in a rice cooker for 20

minutes or until they are cooked through and soft. *(6)* Garnish with mint chutney and serve hot with naan bread.

85. CHICKEN CAPELLINI

Total Time: 30 minutes | Prep Time: 10 minutes

Ingredients:

200g capellini pasta

1 tablespoon olive oil

1/2 cup cherry tomatoes, halved

Salt and pepper to taste

250g chicken breast, thinly sliced

2 cloves garlic, minced

1/4 cup fresh basil leaves, chopped

Grated Parmesan cheese for garnish

Directions:

(1) In a rice cooker, prepare pasta with capellini following the manufacturer's instructions. *(2)* In a skillet set over middle heat, warm the olive oil. Sauté the minced garlic until it releases its aroma. *(3)* In a pan over medium heat, sauté the sliced chicken breast until it becomes white. *(4)* Toss the cooked pasta into the pan with the chicken after it's done cooking. *(5)* Add the fresh basil leaves and cherry tomatoes. Add a little salt & pepper to taste. *(6)* Warm the dish and top it with grated Parmesan cheese before serving

86. CHICKEN CROXETTI

Total Time: 30 minutes | Prep Time: 10 minutes

Ingredients:

1 cup croxetti pasta

1 tablespoon butter

2 tablespoons chopped parsley

Lemon wedges for serving

250g chicken thighs, diced

1 tablespoon lemon juice

Salt and pepper to taste

Directions:

(1) Follow the manufacturer's directions for cooking croxetti pasta in a rice cooker. *(2)* Butter should be melted over medium heat in a separate skillet. *(3)* Toss in some chopped chicken thighs and sear them until they're browned and cooked through. *(4)* After the pasta is done cooking, toss it into the pan with the chicken. *(5)* Pour the lemon juice over the spaghetti and chicken. Top with some finely chopped parsley. *(6)* Taste & add salt & pepper as needed. *(7)* Warm the dish and garnish with lemon wedges.

87. SPANAKOPITA

Total Time: 30 minutes | Prep Time: 10 minutes

Ingredients:

1 cup chopped spinach

1/4 cup chopped red onion

1/2 cup crumbled feta cheese

1 tablespoon olive oil

1 teaspoon dried oregano

4 sheets of phyllo pastry, thawed

Salt and pepper to taste

Cooking spray

Directions:

(1) Shake together chopped spinach, crumbled feta cheese, diced red onion, olive oil, dried oregano, salt, and pepper in a mixing bowl. (2) Square up the sheets of phyllo pastry. (3) On top of each phyllo piece, pour some spinach mixture. (4) Seal the edges of the triangles formed by folding the phyllo squares diagonally. (5) Apply a thin layer of cooking spray to the pot of the rice cooker. (6) Set the rice cooker pot in a triangular shape with the spanakopita. (7) After ten to fifteen minutes of cooking time, the rice should be crispy and golden brown. (8) Warm up and enjoy as a snack or appetizer.

88. STUFFED MUSHROOMS

Total Time: 30 minutes | Prep Time: 10 minutes

Ingredients:

8 large mushrooms, stems removed and finely chopped	1/2 cup breadcrumbs
1/4 cup grated Parmesan cheese	2 cloves garlic, minced
2 tablespoons chopped fresh parsley	Salt and pepper to taste
Olive oil for drizzling	

Directions:

(1) Mash the garlic cloves, add the breadcrumbs, Parmesan cheese, chopped fresh parsley, salt, & pepper to a dish with the cut stems of mushrooms. (2) Put a little of the breadcrumb mixture into each mushroom cap. (3) Toss the filled mushrooms with the olive oil. (4) In the rice cooker, add the filled mushrooms. (5) To make the mushrooms soft, simmer them for around fifteen to twenty minutes in a rice cooker. (6) As a tasty appetizer or side dish, serve hot.

89. FASOLADA

Total Time: 30 minutes | Prep Time: 10 minutes

Ingredients:

1 cup dried white beans	4 cups vegetable broth
1 onion, diced	2 carrots, diced
2 celery stalks, diced	2 cloves garlic, minced
1 can (14 oz) diced tomatoes	1 teaspoon dried oregano
Salt and pepper to taste	Olive oil for drizzling

Directions:

(1) After rinsing them with cold water, drain the white beans. (2) The rice cooker should be filled with white beans, vegetable broth, chopped onion, carrots, celery, minced garlic, diced tomatoes, dried oregano, salt, and pepper. (3) Press the "Quick Cook" or "Soup" button on the rice cooker and cover it. (4) Just 20 minutes of cooking time should be enough to soften the beans in the fasolada. (5) Pour olive oil over cooked food just before serving. (6) Alright, the next recipe is up next.

90. CHICKEN BAKED ZITI

Total Time: 30 minutes | Prep Time: 10 minutes

Ingredients:

2 cups ziti pasta	1 cup marinara sauce
1 cup cooked chicken,	1 cup shredded
shredded	mozzarella cheese
1/2 cup grated Parmesan cheese	1 teaspoon dried basil

Salt and pepper to taste

(1) Make sure the ziti pasta is cooked al dente per the package directions. Rinse and reserve. **(2)** Layer the cooked ziti pasta, marinara sauce, shredded chicken, mozzarella cheese, Parmesan cheese, dried basil, salt, and pepper in the rice cooker pot in equal portions. Repeat with the remaining pasta and sauce. **(3)** Layer the remaining ingredients in the same way. **(4)** Lock the rice cooker's cover and choose the "Bake" or "Quick Cook" option. **(5)** After 20 minutes of baking, the chicken baked ziti should be bubbling and the cheese melted. **(6)** Warm up and savor!

91.   CHICKEN ORZO

Total Time: 30 minutes | Prep Time: 10 minutes

Ingredients:

1 cup orzo pasta	2 cups chicken broth
1 cup cooked chicken, diced	1 cup spinach leaves
1/4 cup grated Parmesan cheese	1 tablespoon lemon juice
Salt and pepper to taste	

Directions:

(1) Before draining, give the orzo pasta a quick rinse in cold water. **(2)** Pasta with orzo, chicken broth, chopped chicken, spinach, Parmesan cheese, lemon juice, salt, and pepper should all be cooked in a rice cooker. **(3)** Turn the rice cooker to the "Risotto" or "Quick Cook" option and cover the pot. **(4)** Twenty minutes should be enough time for the orzo to get soft and soak up all of the chicken orzo's liquid. **(5)** Before you serve the chicken orzo, fluff it with a fork. **(6)** The last step is to draft the instructions for the fourth dish.

92.   CHICKEN CONCHIGLIE

Total Time: 30 minutes | Prep Time: 10 minutes

Ingredients:

2 cups conchiglie pasta	2 cups chicken broth
1 cup cooked chicken, chopped	1 cup broccoli florets
1/2 cup heavy cream	1/4 cup grated Parmesan cheese
2 tablespoons chopped fresh parsley	Salt and pepper to taste

Directions:

(1) Make sure the conchiglie pasta is cooked al dente per the package directions. Rinse and reserve. **(2)** Boil the conchiglie pasta according to package directions. Add chicken stock, broccoli florets, chopped parsley, heavy cream, grated Parmesan cheese, and pepper to the rice cooker. Cook until pasta is al dente. **(3)** After placing the cover back on the rice cooker, turn it to the "Risotto" or "Quick Cook" option. **(4)** Twenty minutes is about right for cooking chicken conchiglie or when pasta is al dente, and the sauce is thick and creamy. **(5)** If preferred, top with more Parmesan and parsley and serve hot.

93.   CHICKEN TORTELLINI

Total Time: 30 minutes | Prep Time: 10 minutes

Ingredients:

1 cup chicken broth	1 cup water
1 cup cheese tortellini	1/2 cup cooked

1/2 cup diced tomatoes

Salt and pepper to taste

chicken, diced

1/4 cup chopped spinach

Directions:

(1) Add water and chicken broth to the rice cooker. (2) Chop some spinach, cut some tomatoes, and add some chicken and cheese tortellini. (3) Add a little salt & pepper to taste. (4) Turn the rice cooker on to the "Cook" or "White Rice" option and cover the lid. (5) Gently remove the cover and stir the mixture once the cooking cycle ends. (6) Warm up and savor!

94. CARROT GINGER SOUP

Total Time: 30 minutes | Prep Time: 10 minutes

Ingredients:

1 tablespoon olive oil

4 large carrots, peeled and chopped

3 cups vegetable broth

1 onion, chopped

1 tablespoon fresh ginger, minced

Salt and pepper to taste

Directions:

(1) To warm the olive oil, use the "Sauté" setting on the rice cooker. (2) Proceed to sauté the chopped onion until it becomes translucent. (3) After two or three minutes , add the minced ginger and diced carrots and continue to sauté. (4) After adding the veggie broth, add salt and pepper to taste. (5) For 20 minutes, with the lid closed, make the rice in a rice cooker on the "Soup" or "Slow Cook" mode. (6) When the cooking cycle is done, puree the soup using a hand blender. (7) Hot serving recommended; adjust spice as needed.

95. CHICKEN CORDON BLEU

Total Time: 30 minutes | Prep Time: 15 minutes

Ingredients:

2 boneless, skinless chicken breasts

4 slices Swiss cheese

1 egg, beaten

4 slices ham

1/2 cup bread crumbs

Salt and pepper to taste

Directions:

(1) In a plastic bag, pound the chicken breasts until they are flat. (2) Pepper and salt the chicken breasts. (3) Top each chicken breast with a ham slice and a Swiss cheese slice. (4) Take the chicken breasts and roll them up so the filling is inside. Use toothpicks to keep them in place. (5) Coat each chicken roll with bread crumbs after dipping it in a beaten egg. (6) Throw the chicken rolls into the rice cooker. (7) After 20 minutes , cover the rice cooker and cook it in "Bake" or "Steam" mode. (8) After the rice cooker's cooking cycle is over, take the chicken rolls out with care, throw away the toothpicks, and cut them into slices. (9) Top with your preferred side and serve hot.

96. PASTRAMI SANDWICH

Total Time: 15 minutes | Prep Time: 5 minutes

Ingredients:

4 slices rye bread

8 slices pastrami

4 slices Swiss cheese
2 tablespoons Thousand Island dressing

1/4 cup sauerkraut

Directions:

(1) Spread out two pieces of rye bread. (2) Spoon sauerkraut, Swiss cheese, and pastrami onto separate slices. (3) Top each sandwich with two pieces of rye bread that have been spread with Thousand Island dressing. (4) Place the sandwich pieces delicately in the rice cooker. (5) Ten minutes later, with the lid closed, put the rice cooker on the "Grill" or "Panini" mode. (6) After the rice cooker's cooking cycle is finished, gently take the sandwiches out and serve them hot.

97.   CHICKEN BUCATINI

Total Time: 25 minutes | Prep Time: 10 minutes

Ingredients:

250g bucatini pasta
2 boneless, skinless chicken breasts, sliced
2 cloves garlic, minced
1/2 cup grated Parmesan cheese

1 tablespoon olive oil
1 onion, diced

1 cup cherry tomatoes, halved
Salt and pepper to taste

Directions:

(1) Make sure to follow the package directions while cooking bucatini. (2) Warm the olive oil in a big skillet over medium heat. Cook the chicken for around 5 minutes or until it becomes brown. (3) Saute the garlic and onion for three minutes or until they are tender. (4) Add cooked pasta and cherry tomatoes and stir to combine. Finish cooking for a further two or three minutes. (5) Take it off the stove, top it with Parmesan, and add some salt and pepper. (6) Hot is best.

98.   AVGOLEMONO SOUP

Total Time: 30 minutes | Prep Time: 10 minutes

Ingredients:

4 cups chicken broth
2 eggs
Salt and pepper to taste

1/2 cup orzo pasta
Juice of 2 lemons

Directions:

(1) Pasta and chicken broth should be combined in a rice cooker. (2) About 20 minutes is the recommended cooking time for rice in a rice cooker. (3) Eggs and lemon juice should be whisked until they form a foam in a bowl. (4) While the orzo cooks, gradually add the egg mixture to the rice cooker, stirring constantly. (5) Taste & add salt & pepper as needed. (6) Hot is best.

99.   BEEF AND BROCCOLI

Total Time: 25 minutes | Prep Time: 10 minutes

Ingredients:

1 pound flank steak, thinly sliced
1/4 cup soy sauce

2 cloves garlic,

2 cups broccoli florets

2 tablespoons brown sugar
1 tablespoon

minced
2 tablespoons water

cornstarch
Cooked rice for serving

Directions:

(1) Combine the garlic, brown sugar, and soy sauce in a small dish. (2) Throw some broccoli

florets and cut flank steak into the rice cooker. **(3)** Add the broccoli and meat to the bowl with the soy sauce. After 15 minutes of cooking using the "quick cook" option, cover the rice cooker and turn it off. **(4)** Prepare a slurry by combining cornstarch and water in an additional basin. Add the slurry to the rice cooker with the meat and broccoli. Stir to combine. **(5)** Make sure the sauce has thickened by continuing to heat for another 5 minutes. **(6)** Heat and serve with cooked rice.

100.   CHICKEN TORTILLA SOUP

Total Time: 30 minutes | Prep Time: 10 minutes

Ingredients:

1 tablespoon olive oil	1 onion, diced
2 cloves garlic, minced	1 teaspoon ground cumin
1 teaspoon chili powder	4 cups chicken broth
1 can diced tomatoes	1 cup frozen corn kernels
1 cup cooked shredded chicken	Salt and pepper to taste
Tortilla chips for serving	Shredded cheese for serving

Directions:

(1) Warm the olive oil in a rice cooker over medium heat. Sauté the garlic and onion for around three minutes or until they are tender. **(2)** Add chile powder and ground cumin, stir, and continue cooking for one more minute. **(3)** To the rice cooker, add chicken broth, corn kernels, chopped tomatoes, and shredded chicken. **(4)** Ten minutes of cooking time on the "soup" option in a covered rice cooker should do the trick. **(5)** Add salt and pepper after cooking, according to your preference. **(6)** Top with grated cheese and tortilla chips and serve hot.

101.   BUFFALO CHICKEN WRAP

Total Time: 25 minutes | Prep Time: 15 minutes

Ingredients:

2 boneless, skinless chicken breasts	1/4 cup buffalo sauce
2 large tortillas	1/2 cup shredded lettuce
1/4 cup diced tomatoes	1/4 cup diced red onion
1/4 cup crumbled blue cheese	Ranch or blue cheese dressing (optional)

Directions:

(1) Before steaming the chicken breasts in a rice cooker with buffalo sauce for 10 minutes , season them with salt and pepper. **(2)** Before shredding the chicken using two forks, take it out of the rice cooker. **(3)** Just two minutes in a rice cooker will warm the tortillas. **(4)** Top each tortilla with blue cheese, red onion, lettuce, tomatoes, and shredded chicken. **(5)** If desired, drizzle with dressing before firmly wrapping and serving.

102.   GREEK YOGURT WITH HONEY AND NUTS

Total Time: 5 minutes | Prep Time: 5 minutes

Ingredients:

1 cup Greek yogurt	2 tablespoons honey
1/4 cup mixed nuts	

Directions:

(1) Spoon Greek yogurt into serving bowls. **(2)** Drizzle honey over the yogurt. **(3)**

Sprinkle mixed nuts on top. *(4)* Serve immediately.

103.   EGG SALAD

Total Time: 20 minutes | Prep Time: 10 minutes

Ingredients:

4 eggs	2 tablespoons mayonnaise
1 teaspoon Dijon mustard	1/4 cup chopped celery
1/4 cup chopped green onions	Salt and pepper to taste

Directions:

(1) Put the eggs and water into the rice cooker. Ten minutes of steaming cooking time should do it. *(2)* After taking the eggs out of the rice cooker, set them aside to cool. To prepare eggs, peel and cut them. *(3)* Chop the eggs and combine them with the mayonnaise, Dijon mustard, celery, and green onions in a bowl. *(4)* Taste & add salt & pepper as needed. *(5)* Top a bed of lettuce with it or use it as a stuffing for sandwiches.

104.   CHICKEN FETTUCCINE ALFREDO

Total Time: 30 minutes | Prep Time: 10 minutes

Ingredients:

8 ounces fettuccine pasta	2 boneless, skinless chicken breasts
2 cups chicken broth	1 cup heavy cream
1 cup grated Parmesan cheese	Salt and pepper to taste

Directions:

(1) Cook the fettuccine noodles in the rice cooker with the chicken stock and the chicken chunks. Make sure the chicken is cooked through and the pasta is al dente by steaming it for 15 minutes . *(2)* Make sure the rice cooker is completely dry before continuing. *(3)* Incorporate the heavy cream and Parmesan cheese into the thickened sauce by stirring until combined. *(4)* Taste & add salt & pepper as needed. *(5)* Warm the dish before serving and top with more Parmesan cheese, if preferred.

105.   CHICKEN FUSILLI

Total Time: 30 minutes | Prep Time: 10 minutes

Ingredients:

250g fusilli pasta	2 chicken breasts, diced
1 tablespoon olive oil	2 cloves garlic, minced
1 onion, chopped	1 red bell pepper, diced
1 can (400g) diced tomatoes	1 teaspoon dried oregano
Salt and pepper to taste	Grated Parmesan cheese for serving (optional)

Directions:

(1) To get an al dente texture, cook the fusilli as directed on the box. Rinse and reserve. *(2)* Warm the olive oil in the rice cooker using the sauté function. Chopped chicken breasts and minced garlic are added. The chicken should be cooked until it becomes golden brown. *(3)* Include the red bell pepper and onion that have been chopped. Keep sautéing until the veggies become soft. *(4)* Add the dried oregano, salt, pepper, and chopped tomatoes and stir to combine. Put the rice cooker on high heat for 10 minutes with the lid closed.

(5) Before the rice cooker timer goes off, cook the fusilli. Mix thoroughly. *(6)* While still heated, top with grated Parmesan cheese if desired.

106. CHICKEN AND SAUSAGE GUMBO

Total Time: 30 minutes | Prep Time: 15 minutes

Ingredients:

1 cup long-grain white rice	2 chicken thighs, boneless and skinless, diced
2 sausages (such as Andouille), sliced	1 tablespoon vegetable oil
1 onion, diced	1 green bell pepper, diced
2 celery stalks, diced	2 cloves garlic, minced
1 can (400g) diced tomatoes	2 cups chicken broth
1 teaspoon Cajun seasoning	Salt and pepper to taste
Chopped parsley for garnish	

Directions:

(1) Make sure the water flows clean after rinsing the rice with cold water. Rinse and reserve. *(2)* Sauté the onion and garlic in the rice cooker until they begin to brown. Sliced sausages and diced chicken thighs should be added. Brown the meat. *(3)* Toss in some chopped celery, green bell pepper, onion, and garlic. Saute the veggies in oil until they're tender. *(4)* Add the chicken broth, chopped tomatoes, Cajun spice, salt, and pepper. Stir to combine. Put the rice cooker on high heat for 15 minutes with the lid closed. *(5)* At the end of the cooking time, fluff the rice and serve the gumbo hot with chopped parsley as a garnish.

107. LAMB SOUVLAKI

Total Time: 30 minutes | Prep Time: 10 minutes

Ingredients:

400g lamb shoulder, cubed	2 tablespoons olive oil
2 tablespoons lemon juice	2 cloves garlic, minced
1 teaspoon dried oregano	Salt and pepper to taste
Pita bread for serving	Tzatziki sauce for serving
Sliced tomatoes, cucumbers, and red onions for serving	

Directions:

(1) Mix the lemon juice, olive oil, salt, pepper, minced garlic, and dried oregano in a bowl. *(2)* Coat the lamb shoulder cubes by adding them to the basin and mixing. Allow it to soak for five minutes . *(3)* Start the rice cooker and put it on sauté to heat it up. Brown the lamb cubes in the marinade before adding them to the pan. *(4)* Put the rice cooker on high heat for 10 minutes with the lid closed. *(5)* Garnish the cooked lamb with sliced tomatoes, cucumbers, and red onions, and serve hot with pita bread and tzatziki sauce.

108. BALSAMIC GLAZED CHICKEN

Total Time: 30 minutes | Prep Time: 10 minutes

Ingredients:

	1 tablespoon honey	1 tablespoon soy sauce
4 chicken drumsticks	2 tablespoons balsamic vinegar	2 cloves garlic, minced	Salt and pepper to taste

Chopped fresh
parsley for garnish

Directions:

(1) Take a mixing bowl and mix together the honey, balsamic vinegar, soy sauce, garlic powder, salt & pepper. **(2)** Then, throw in the chicken drumsticks to coat. Allow it to soak for five minutes . **(3)** Start the rice cooker and put it on sauté to heat it up. After the marinade has been applied, brown the chicken drumsticks on both sides. **(4)** Put the rice cooker on high heat for 15 minutes with the lid closed. **(5)** Finish cooking the chicken and thickening the sauce. Garnish with chopped fresh parsley & serve hot.

109.   SMOKED S M,C BNBVC BNM SALMON

Total Time: 30 minutes | Prep Time: 10 minutes

Ingredients:

1 cup rice
200g smoked salmon, sliced
2 tablespoons chopped fresh dill

1 ½ cups water
1 tablespoon lemon juice
Salt and pepper to taste

Directions:

(1) After rinsing the rice, add it to the rice cooker with the water. Cover & cook on high warm for 10 minutes . **(2)** Once cooked, fluff the rice with a fork & transfer it to a serving dish. **(3)** Top with sliced smoked salmon. **(4)** Drizzle lemon juice over the salmon and sprinkle chopped dill. **(5)** Season with salt & pepper to taste. **(6)** Serve immediately and savor the smoked salmon rice bowl!

110.   CHICKEN SPAGHETTI

Total Time: 30 minutes | Prep Time: 10 minutes

Ingredients:

1 cup spaghetti, broken into halves
1 chicken breast, diced
1/2 cup diced bell peppers
2 cloves garlic, minced
Salt and pepper to taste

2 cups water
1 cup diced tomatoes
1/4 cup chopped onions
1 teaspoon Italian seasoning

Directions:

(1) Pound or dice the chicken breast, then add it to the rice cooker with the pasta, water, tomatoes, peppers, onions, garlic, Italian seasoning, salt, and pepper. **(2)** Put the rice cooker on high heat and cover it. **(3)** After the pasta and chicken are cooked and soft, give the mixture a good toss. **(4)** If necessary, make adjustments to the seasoning. **(5)** Enjoy your hot, flavorful chicken spaghetti right out of the rice   cooker!

111.   CORN CHOWDER

Total Time: 30 minutes | Prep Time: 10 minutes

Ingredients:

1 cup corn kernels
1 potato, diced
1/4 cup diced celery
1/2 cup milk

2 cups chicken broth
1/2 cup diced carrots
1/4 cup diced onions
2 tablespoons all-

purpose flour

Salt and pepper to taste

Directions:

(1) Throw in some chopped onion, carrots, celery, chicken stock, corn kernels, and diced potato to the rice cooker. **(2)** Put the rice cooker on high heat and cover it. **(3)** Make a slurry by combining the flour and milk in a different bowl. **(4)** After the veggies are soft, add the slurry to the rice cooker and stir to combine. **(5)** Keep simmering until the chowder reaches the desired consistency. **(6)** Taste & add salt & pepper as needed. **(7)** If preferred, sprinkle with chopped parsley and serve hot.

112.   CHICKEN CANNELLONI

Total Time: 30 minutes | Prep Time: 10 minutes

Ingredients:

6 cannelloni tubes	1 cup cooked shredded chicken
1 cup marinara sauce	1/2 cup ricotta cheese
1/4 cup grated Parmesan cheese	1/2 teaspoon dried oregano
Salt and pepper to taste	

Directions:

(1) Gather the chicken, ricotta, Parmesan, dried oregano, salt, & pepper in a bowl & combine. **(2)** Gather the chicken ingredients and stuff the cannelloni tubes. **(3)** Before you start cooking the rice, pour in half of the marinara sauce. **(4)** After the sauce has been added, arrange the filled cannelloni tubes on top. **(5)** Top the cannelloni with the rest of the marinara sauce. **(6)** Put the rice cooker on high heat and cover it. **(7)** Serve immediately after the cannelloni has cooked and the sauce has bubbled. **(8)** For garnish, feel free to add a little more Parmesan cheese just before serving.

113.   CHICKEN STUFFED SHELLS

Total Time: 30 minutes | Prep Time: 10 minutes

Ingredients:

12 jumbo pasta shells	1 cup cooked chicken, shredded
1 cup ricotta cheese	1/2 cup grated Parmesan cheese
1/2 cup marinara sauce	1/4 teaspoon garlic powder
Salt and pepper to taste	

Directions:

Make sure the giant pasta shells are cooked al dente as directed on the packet. Rinse and reserve. **(2)** Get a bowl and throw in some shredded chicken, ricotta, Parmesan, garlic powder, salt, and pepper. Mix well. **(3)** Spoon the chicken and cheese mixture into the prepared pasta shells. **(4)** Spread marinara sauce evenly over the bottom of the rice cooker pot. **(5)** Put the filled shells in the saucepan. **(6)** Top the shells with the rest of the marinara sauce. **(7)** After adding the rice, cover the cooker and cook for 15 minutes using the "Quick Cook" option. **(8)** Give it a few minutes to rest when cooking is complete. I hope you enjoy these Chicken Stuffed Shells.

114. CHICKEN NOODLE SOUP

Total Time: 30 minutes | Prep Time: 10 minutes

Ingredients:

2 cups cooked chicken, shredded
1 cup egg noodles
1 celery stalk, chopped
2 cloves garlic, minced
Salt and pepper to taste

4 cups chicken broth

1 carrot, sliced
½ onion, diced

1 teaspoon dried thyme

Directions:

Sauté the onion, carrot, celery, garlic, and dried thyme in the rice cooker pot with the chicken stock. *(2)* After adding the rice, cover and simmer for 10 minutes on the "Soup" option in the rice cooker. *(3)* When the veggies are almost done cooking, throw in the egg noodles and shredded chicken. *(4)* Reset the rice cooker to "Quick Cook" & cover it again; cook for 10 more minutes. *(5)* Before serving, season with salt and pepper according to your taste. My Chicken Noodle Soup is Delicious!

115. CHICKEN DIAVOLO

Total Time: 30 minutes | Prep Time: 10 minutes

Ingredients:

4 boneless, skinless chicken breasts
3 cloves garlic, minced
1 can (14 oz) diced tomatoes
Salt and pepper to taste

1/4 cup olive oil

1 teaspoon crushed red pepper flakes
1/4 cup chopped fresh basil

Directions:

(1) Pepper and salt the chicken breasts. *(2)* Add the minced garlic and olive oil to the rice cooker pot and heat them up using the "Saute" mode. *(3)* After one more minute, stir in the crushed red pepper flakes. *(4)* Cook the chicken breasts in a skillet until they are browned all over. *(5)* Top the chicken with chopped tomatoes. *(6)* After adding the rice, cover the cooker and cook for 15 minutes on the "Chicken" option. *(7)* After the chicken is cooked, garnish it with chopped fresh basil and serve. Chicken Diavolo is delicious.

116. CHICKEN PESTO

Total Time: 30 minutes | Prep Time: 10 minutes

Ingredients:

4 boneless, skinless chicken breasts
1/4 cup grated Parmesan cheese

1/2 cup pesto sauce

Salt and pepper to taste

Directions:

(1) Pepper and salt the chicken breasts. *(2)* Apply a thin coating of pesto sauce to the saucepan of the rice cooker. *(3)* Top the pesto sauce with the chicken breasts. *(4)* Coat the chicken breasts with the leftover pesto sauce. *(5)* After 20 minutes of cooking on the "Chicken" option, cover the rice cooker and turn it off. *(6)* Before serving, top the chicken with grated Parmesan cheese. The Chicken Pesto is delicious.

117.   LAMB ROGAN JOSH

Total Time: 30 minutes | Prep Time: 10 minutes

Ingredients:

1 lb lamb, diced	2 tbsp vegetable oil
1 onion, finely chopped	2 cloves garlic, minced
1 tbsp ginger, grated	2 tbsp Rogan Josh spice blend
1 cup canned diced tomatoes	1 cup water or broth
Salt to taste	Fresh cilantro for garnish (optional)

Directions:

(1) Use the "Sauté" setting on your rice cooker to heat up some vegetable oil. **(2)** Brown the lamb dice in the pan for about 5 minutes or until browned all over. **(3)** Grated ginger, minced garlic, and chopped onion should be added. Let the onions soften and become transparent while cooking. **(4)** To unleash the flavors, stir in the Rogan Josh spice combination and simmer for an additional minute. **(5)** Pour in the water or broth, chopped tomatoes from a can, and salt to taste. **(6)** After 15 minutes of sealing the lid, switch to "Manual" or "Pressure Cook" mode on the rice cooker. **(7)** Then, after a few minutes of natural pressure release, open the lid. **(8)** Serve immediately with hot rice or naan and, if wanted, garnish with fresh cilantro.

118.   TURKEY CLUB SANDWICH

Total Time: 15 minutes | Prep Time: 5 minutes

Ingredients:

4 slices of bread	6 slices of turkey breast
4 slices of cooked bacon	2 leaves of lettuce
2 slices of tomato	Mayonnaise
Mustard	Salt and pepper to taste

Directions:

(1) Layer turkey breast, bacon, lettuce, and tomato on top of two pieces of bread in the rice cooker. **(2)** Sandwich the remaining two pieces of bread together with the mayonnaise and mustard. **(3)** For 5 minutes , or until the bread is toasted and the sandwich is cooked through, close the lid of the rice cooker and choose the "Grill" or "Toast" setting. **(4)** Before serving, carefully take the sandwiches out of the rice cooker. If preferred, cut them in half.

119.   CHICKEN AND WAFFLES

Total Time: 30 minutes | Prep Time: 10 minutes

Ingredients:

4 frozen chicken tenders	2 frozen waffles
Maple syrup	Butter

Directions:

(1) Use the "Grill" or "Bake" setting on the rice cooker to get it ready to cook. **(2)** To get frozen chicken tenders crispy and cooked through, toss them in a rice cooker & cook for ten to twelve minutes , turning once halfway through. **(3)** Get the frozen waffles crispy and golden brown in the toaster while the chicken cooks. **(4)** Take the chicken tenders out of the rice cooker when they are done cooking and put them aside. **(5)** To reheat, throw the toasted waffles into the rice cooker and let them cook for another two or three minutes. **(6)** Put the chicken tenders on top of the waffles, then pour maple syrup over them. If you like, you can also put some butter on top.

120.   CHICKEN SORRENTINA

Total Time: 30 minutes | Prep Time: 10 minutes

Ingredients:

2 boneless, skinless chicken breasts

1 cup marinara sauce

1/4 cup grated Parmesan cheese

Salt and pepper to taste

1 cup shredded mozzarella cheese

Fresh basil leaves for garnish (optional)

Directions:

(1) Put some salt and pepper on the chicken breasts & season them on both sides. *(2)* Get the rice cooker hot by pressing the "Sauté" button. *(3)* Sear the chicken breasts in a rice cooker for two or three minutes on each side or until they get a golden brown color. *(4)* After coating the chicken breasts with marinara sauce, top with shredded mozzarella cheese. *(5)* Cook the chicken until it's done and the cheese is melted and bubbling. Cover the rice cooker and put it on "Bake" or "Cook" mode for 15 minutes. *(6)* Garnish the chicken breasts with fresh basil leaves and grated Parmesan cheese after they are done. *(7)* Accompany with hot spaghetti or salad for a side dish.

121.   POACHED SALMON

Total Time: 25 minutes | Prep Time: 5 minutes

Ingredients:

4 salmon fillets

1 lemon, sliced

4 cups water

Salt and pepper to taste

Directions:

(1) Put some lemon slices and water in the rice cooker. *(2)* Add salt & pepper to the salmon fillets. *(3)* Place the salmon fillets delicately into the rice cooker. *(4)* After adding the rice to the cooker, cover it and cook it for 20 minutes . *(5)* Carefully take the salmon fillets out of the rice cooker when done, and serve immediately.

122.   SEVEN LAYER DIP

Total Time: 30 minutes | Prep Time: 10 minutes

Ingredients:

1 can of refried beans

1 cup guacamole

1 cup shredded cheese

1/4 cup sliced black olives

1 cup sour cream

1 cup salsa

1/2 cup chopped tomatoes

Tortilla chips for dipping

Directions:

(1) Spread the refried beans out evenly in the rice cooker's base. *(2)* Top the beans with the sour cream. *(3)* Spoon guacamole over the sour cream as a topping. *(4)* Top with salsa and guacamole. *(5)* On top of the salsa, equally distribute the shredded cheese. *(6)* Grated black olives and diced tomatoes make a tasty topping. *(7)* After 20 minutes of warming, cover the rice cooker. *(8)* Accompany with tortilla chips.

123. CHICKEN TORTIGLIONI

Total Time: 30 minutes | Prep Time: 10 minutes

Ingredients:

2 chicken breasts, diced

2 cups chicken broth

1/2 cup diced onions

2 cloves garlic, minced

2 cups tortiglioni pasta

1 cup marinara sauce

1/2 cup diced bell peppers

Salt and pepper to taste

Directions:

(1) Toss the tortellini pasta with the diced chicken, chicken stock, marinara sauce, chopped onions and peppers, garlic, and salt and pepper in a rice cooker. *(2)* After adding the rice to the cooker, cover it and cook it for 20 minutes . *(3)* After it's done, mix it briefly and serve it hot.

124. HONEY GARLIC SALMON

Total Time: 25 minutes | Prep Time: 5 minutes

Ingredients:

4 salmon fillets

2 tablespoons soy sauce

1 tablespoon olive oil

1/4 cup honey

2 cloves garlic, minced

Salt and pepper to taste

Directions:

(1) Combine the honey, soy sauce, olive oil, minced garlic, salt, & pepper in a little bowl and whisk to combine. *(2)* In a rice cooker, add the salmon fillets. *(3)* Make sure the salmon fillets are covered evenly with the honey garlic sauce before serving. *(4)* After adding the rice to the cooker, cover it and cook it for 20 minutes . *(5)* Carefully take the salmon fillets out of the rice cooker when done, and serve immediately.

125. CHICKEN AND DUMPLINGS

Total Time: 30 minutes | Prep Time: 10 minutes

Ingredients:

2 boneless, skinless chicken breasts, diced

1 cup diced celery

2 cloves garlic, minced

1 cup frozen peas

1/3 cup milk

1 cup diced carrots

1 onion, diced

4 cups chicken broth

1 cup biscuit mix

Directions:

(1) Toss the chicken, celery, carrots, onion, garlic, and chicken stock into the rice cooker. *(2)* Lock the lid and choose "Soup" or "Stew" as the cooking mode for the rice cooker. Finish cooking after 20 minutes . *(3)* Prepare the biscuit dough by combining the biscuit mix with the milk in a separate dish while the soup is simmering. *(4)* Remove the cover and mix in the frozen peas after 20 minutes. *(5)* Add crumbled biscuit dough to the broth by spoonfuls. *(6)* Once the dumplings are halfway done cooking, cover and simmer for another 10 minutes. Hot is best.

126. BEEF BARLEY SOUP

Total Time: 30 minutes | Prep Time: 10 minutes

Ingredients:

1 pound beef stew meat, cubed

1 onion, diced

2 cloves garlic, minced	1 cup diced carrots
1 cup diced celery	1 cup pearl barley
4 cups beef broth	Salt and pepper to taste

(1) Put the barley, beef broth, onion, garlic, carrots, and celery into the rice cooker. Add the beef stew meat. *(2)* Add a little salt & pepper to taste. *(3)* Lock the lid and choose "Soup" or "Stew" as the cooking mode for the rice cooker. *(4)* Allow to cook for 90 minutes . *(5)* Hot is best.

127.   PORK CHOPS

Total Time: 25 minutes | Prep Time: 5 minutes

Ingredients:

4 pork chops	Salt and pepper to taste
1 tablespoon olive oil	

Directions:

(1) Pepper and salt the pork chops. *(2)* Warm the olive oil in the rice cooker by turning it on the "Saute" setting. *(3)* The pork chops should be sautéed in heated oil for 10 minutes , turning once, or until browned and cooked through. *(4)* Hot is best.

128.   PISTACHIO-CRUSTED SALMON

Total Time: 20 minutes | Prep Time: 5 minutes

Ingredients:

4 salmon fillets	Salt and pepper to taste
1/2 cup chopped pistachios	2 tablespoons Dijon mustard

Directions:

(1) Add salt & pepper to the salmon fillets. *(2)* Top each fillet with a generous coating of Dijon mustard. *(3)* After coating the fish with mustard, press chopped pistachios onto it. *(4)* Lay a foil or parchment paper layer in the rice cooker. *(5)* Spread out the parchment paper or aluminum foil & place the salmon fillets on top. *(6)* After placing the cover back on the rice cooker, turn it to the "Steam" option. After 15 minutes of cooking, the salmon should be opaque throughout and flaky when tested with a fork. Hot is best.

129.   PESTO PASTA

Total Time: 25 minutes | Prep Time: 10 minutes

Ingredients:

200g pasta of your choice (spaghetti, penne, fusilli, etc.)	2 tablespoons pesto sauce
1 tablespoon olive oil	2 cloves garlic, minced
Salt and pepper to taste	Grated Parmesan cheese for serving (optional)

Directions:

(1) Casserole the spaghetti into the rice cooker. *(2)* Toss the spaghetti with enough water to coat it. *(3)* Combine with olive oil, minced garlic, salt, and pepper. *(4)* Turn the rice cooker on high heat and cover it. *(5)* If needed, drain the pasta water after cooking. *(6)* Blend in the pesto sauce by stirring well. *(7)*

If preferred, serve hot with grated Parmesan cheese as a garnish.

130. PASTITSIO

Total Time: 30 minutes | Prep Time: 10 minutes

Ingredients:

200g penne pasta	250g ground beef
1 onion, chopped	2 cloves garlic, minced
1 cup tomato sauce	1 teaspoon dried oregano
1 teaspoon dried basil	Salt and pepper to taste
1 cup shredded mozzarella cheese	

Directions:

(1) Follow the package directions for cooking penne pasta in a rice cooker. (2) Brown the ground beef in another skillet with the chopped onions and minced garlic. (3) Season the meat mixture with salt, pepper, dried basil, oregano, and tomato sauce. Allow to cook for a duration of 5 minutes . (4) Put half of the cooked pasta into the rice cooker pot. (5) Dump half of the meat mixture onto the spaghetti. (6) Layer the leftover meat and noodle mixture again. (7) Grated mozzarella cheese may be sprinkled on top. (8) After adding the cheese, cover the rice cooker and simmer until the cheese melts and begins to bubble. (9) Hot is best.

131. CHICKEN CHOPS

Total Time: 30 minutes | Prep Time: 10 minutes

Ingredients:

4 boneless chicken chops	2 tablespoons olive oil
2 cloves garlic, minced	1 teaspoon paprika
1 teaspoon dried thyme	Salt and pepper to taste

Directions:

(1) Add salt, pepper, paprika, dry thyme, and chopped garlic to the chicken chops. (2) Before using, heat the olive oil in a pan over middle-warm heat. (3) To get a golden brown crust, sear the chicken chops for two to three minutes on each side. (4) Place the chicken chops that have been seared in the rice cooker. (5) After adding the chicken, cover the rice cooker and cook on high heat until the chicken is done. (6) Then top with your preferred accompaniments and serve hot.

132. KEFTEDES

Total Time: 30 minutes | Prep Time: 15 minutes

Ingredients:

250g ground beef or lamb	1 small onion, grated
2 cloves garlic, minced	1 teaspoon dried oregano
1 teaspoon dried mint	Salt and pepper to taste
2 tablespoons breadcrumbs	

Directions:

(1) Blend together ground meat (either lamb or beef), finely chopped garlic, dried oregano and mint, breadcrumbs, salt, and pepper in a bowl. (2) Thoroughly combine all ingredients by mixing them together. (3) Make little meatballs using the ingredients. (4) Finish cooking the rice in a saucepan and add the meatballs. (5) Make sure the meatballs are

well cooked before putting them in the rice cooker to boil. *(6)* Garnish with pita bread and tzatziki sauce before serving hot.

133. GRILLED CHEESE SANDWICH

Total Time: 15 minutes | Prep Time: 5 minutes

Ingredients:

4 slices of bread

4 slices of cheddar cheese & Butter

Directions:

(1) On medium heat, warm a pan that doesn't stick. *(2)* Coat each slice of bread with butter. *(3)* Spread butter on both sides of two pieces of bread and lay them on the pan. *(4)* Place a slice of cheese on top of each piece of bread. *(5)* Toast the other half of the bread and lay it on top. *(6)* Flip once the bottom has become golden, & continue cooking until the cheese has melted & the other side has turned golden as well. *(7)* Serve hot after removing from heat.

134. CHICKEN ENCHILADAS

Total Time: 25 minutes | Prep Time: 10 minutes

Ingredients:

2 cups cooked chicken, shredded

1 cup salsa

1 cup shredded cheese

8 small flour tortillas

Optional toppings: sour cream, chopped cilantro, diced tomatoes

Directions:

(1) Use the "Keep Warm" option on your rice cooker to get it ready to cook. *(2)* Combine the salsa with the shredded chicken in a mixing basin. *(3)* Fill each tortilla with a dollop of the chicken mixture and fold them up. *(4)* Roll out the tortillas and set them aside in the rice cooker. *(5)* Before serving, top with shredded cheese. *(6)* Cook, covered, for about 15 minutes or until cheese melts and bubbles. *(7)* Get it hot and top it with anything you want.

135. BUTTERNUT SQUASH SOUP

Total Time: 30 minutes | Prep Time: 10 minutes

Ingredients:

1 small butternut squash, peeled and cubed

1 onion, chopped

2 cloves garlic, minced

4 cups vegetable broth

Salt and pepper to taste

Optional toppings: cream, pumpkin seeds, chopped chives

Directions:

(1) In a rice cooker, combine the cubed butternut squash with the chopped onion, minced garlic, and vegetable broth. *(2)* Put the rice cooker on the "Soup" or "Cook" setting and cover it. *(3)* Squash should be cooked and covered for approximately 20 minutes or until desired softness is achieved. *(4)* Smooth out the soup by pureeing it with an immersion blender. *(5)* Taste & add salt & pepper as needed. *(6)* Get it hot and top it with anything you want.

136.   FISH CURRY

Total Time: 30 minutes | Prep Time: 10 minutes

Ingredients:

1 lb white fish fillets, cut into chunks

1 onion, chopped

2 tomatoes, chopped

1 can of coconut milk

2 tablespoons curry powder

Salt to taste

Fresh cilantro for garnish

Directions:

(1) In a rice cooker, add the chopped tomatoes and onion. *(2)* Top with the fish pieces. *(3)* Drizzle the fish with the coconut milk. *(4)* Season with salt and curry powder. *(5)* Put the rice cooker on the "Cook" setting and cover it. *(6)* The fish should be cooked thoroughly, and the curry should bubble for around 20 minutes . *(7)* Before serving, top with chopped fresh cilantro.

137.   CHICKEN SOUVLAKI

Total Time: 30 minutes | Prep Time: 15 minutes

Ingredients:

1 lb chicken breast, cut into cubes

2 tablespoons olive oil

2 tablespoons lemon juice

2 cloves garlic, minced

1 teaspoon dried oregano

Salt and pepper to taste

Coat the chicken cubes equally by adding them to the marinade and stirring to combine. Ten minutes is all it needs to marinade. *(3)* Set the "Cook" setting on your rice cooker to preheat it. *(4)* After adding the marinated chicken to the rice cooker, heat for about 10 to 12 minutes, stirring regularly, or until the chicken is cooked through. *(5)* Accompany with hot rice or salad.

Directions:

(1) Combine olive oil, lemon juice, garlic, oregano, salt, and pepper in a mixing bowl. *(2)*

138.   TABOULI

Total Time: 20 minutes | Prep Time: 10 minutes

Ingredients:

1 cup bulgur wheat

2 cups water

2 tomatoes, diced

1 cucumber, diced

1/2 cup fresh parsley, chopped

1/4 cup fresh mint leaves, chopped

1/4 cup lemon juice

2 tablespoons olive oil

Salt and pepper to taste

cooker on the "Cook" setting and cover it. After around 10 minutes of cooking, the bulgur should be soft. *(3)* Garnish with mint, parsley, cucumber, lemon juice, olive oil, salt, and pepper. Combine in a separate bowl. *(4)* After the bulgur has cooked, give it a little fluff with a fork and set it aside to cool. *(5)* After the bulgur is cooked, add the vegetable mixture and stir well. *(6)* Tabouli salad may be served either cold or at room temperature.

Directions:

(1) Drain the bulgur wheat after rinsing it with cold water. *(2)* Add the bulgur wheat and water to the rice cooker pot. Put the rice

139. BEEF WRAPS

Total Time: 25 minutes | Prep Time: 15 minutes

Ingredients:

1 lb beef sirloin, thinly sliced

1 bell pepper, thinly sliced

2 tablespoons hoisin sauce

1 teaspoon minced ginger

Tortillas or lettuce leaves for wrapping

1 onion, thinly sliced

2 tablespoons soy sauce

1 teaspoon sesame oil

Salt and pepper to taste

Directions:

(1) Combine ginger, sesame oil, hoisin sauce, soy sauce, salt, and pepper in a bowl. *(2)* After 10 minutes , add the thinly sliced meat to the marinade. *(3)* Set the "Cook" setting on your rice cooker to preheat it. *(4)* Put the bell pepper, onion, and marinated meat in the rice cooker. Stirring periodically, cover, and simmer for eight to ten minutes or until meat is cooked through. *(5)* Fill tortillas or lettuce leaves with the cooked meat mixture and serve as wraps.

140. CRAB CAKES

Total Time: 30 minutes | Prep Time: 10 minutes

Ingredients:

1 lb lump crab meat

1/4 cup mayonnaise

1 egg, beaten

1 tablespoon lemon juice

Salt and pepper to taste

1/2 cup breadcrumbs

2 green onions, finely chopped

1 tablespoon Dijon mustard

1 teaspoon Old Bay seasoning

Directions:

(1) Mix the crab, breadcrumbs, mayo, green onions, egg, Dijon mustard, lemon juice, Old Bay seasoning, salt, and pepper in a big bowl. *(2)* Shape the ingredients into little patties. *(3)* Set the "Cook" setting on your rice cooker to preheat it. *(4)* After adding the crab cakes to the rice cooker, cook for about 10 to 12 minutes , turning once halfway through cooking or until they get a golden brown color and are cooked through. *(5)* Hot crab cakes are best served with a sauce of your choice.

141. CHICKEN CURZETTI

Total Time: 30 minutes | Prep Time: 10 minutes

Ingredients:

1 cup rice

1 cup rice

2 chicken breasts, diced

2 cloves garlic, minced

1 tablespoon olive oil

1 ½ cups chicken broth

1 ½ cups chicken broth

1 onion, chopped

1 bell pepper, diced

1 teaspoon Italian seasoning

Salt and pepper to taste

Directions:

(1) Before adding chicken stock to the rice cooker, rinse the rice. Get the rice cooker going. *(2)* In a pan set over middle heat, warm the olive oil while the rice cooks. Toss in the bell pepper, onion, and garlic. Cook until tender. *(3)* Cook the diced chicken until it is browned and cooked through in the skillet. *(4)*

Add salt, pepper, and Italian seasoning to the chicken. **(5)** After the rice cooker sets to "warm," combine the cooked rice and chicken. **(6)** Warm up and savor!

142. GREEK MEZZE PLATTER

Total Time: 25 minutes | Prep Time: 15 minutes

Ingredients:

1 cup rice	1 ½ cups vegetable broth
1 cucumber, sliced	1 tomato, diced
½ cup feta cheese, crumbled	¼ cup Kalamata olives
2 tablespoons olive oil	1 tablespoon lemon juice
1 teaspoon dried oregano	Salt and pepper to taste

Directions:

(1) After rinsing, add the rice and vegetable broth to the rice cooker. Get the rice cooker going. **(2)** As the rice is simmering, set a serving tray with sliced cucumber, chopped tomato, feta cheese, and Kalamata olives. **(3)** A little bowl will do for the dressing; to create it, mix together the olive oil, lemon juice, dried oregano, salt & pepper. **(4)** When the rice cooker's setting changes to "warm," fluff the rice and pour it into a bowl to serve. **(5)** Once the rice is coated, pour the dressing over it and gently mix to blend. **(6)** Accompany the mezze dish with the rice and savor!

143. CHICKEN SALTIMBOCCA

Total Time: 30 minutes | Prep Time: 10 minutes

Ingredients:

1 cup rice	1 ½ cups chicken broth
2 chicken breasts, pounded thin	4 slices prosciutto
4 slices mozzarella cheese	2 tablespoons olive oil
¼ cup white wine	2 tablespoons butter
Salt and pepper to taste	

Directions:

(1) Before adding chicken stock to the rice cooker, rinse the rice. Get the rice cooker going. **(2)** Add salt & pepper to the chicken breasts while the rice cooks. Use two slices of prosciutto and one piece of mozzarella cheese to encase each chicken breast. **(3)** Olive oil should be heated in a pan over medium-high heat. Add the bundled chicken breasts to the pan after frying the breasts in a skillet until they become golden brown. **(4)** White wine should be used to deglaze the pan, taking care to eliminate any remaining discoloration from the base of the pan. **(5)** After the rice cooker setting turns to "warm," take out the cooked rice and arrange it on plates for dinner. **(6)** Place a chicken saltimbocca breast on top of each plate of rice and top with pan sauce. **(7)** Warm up and savor!

144. CHICKEN CAVATELLI

Total Time: 30 minutes | Prep Time: 10 minutes

Ingredients:

1 cup rice	1 ½ cups chicken broth
2 chicken breasts,	1 cup broccoli florets
thinly sliced	
1 cup sliced mushrooms	1 onion, sliced
2 cloves garlic, minced	2 tablespoons soy sauce

1 tablespoon sesame oil

1 teaspoon ginger, grated

Salt and pepper to taste

Directions:

(1) Before adding chicken stock to the rice cooker, rinse the rice. Get the rice cooker going. **(2)** In a pan, heat the sesame oil over middle heat while the rice is cooking. Brown the cut chicken by adding it to the pan. **(3)** Squeeze in some minced garlic, broccoli florets, and mushrooms once you've cut them. Just until the veggies are soft, cook them. **(4)** Add salt, pepper, grated ginger, soy sauce, and stir. **(5)** When the rice cooker's setting turns to "warm," combine the cooked rice with the chicken and vegetable combination. **(6)** Warm up and savor!

145. CHICKEN SCIALATIELLI

Total Time: 30 minutes | Prep Time: 10 minutes

Ingredients:

1 lb boneless, skinless chicken breasts, diced

1 onion, diced

1 can diced tomatoes

Salt and pepper to taste

1 cup scialatielli pasta

2 cloves garlic, minced

1 teaspoon dried oregano

Directions:

(1) Put the following ingredients in the rice cooker: chicken, scialatielli, onion, garlic, tomatoes, dried oregano, salt, and pepper. Cook until tender. **(2)** Submerge all ingredients by adding water. **(3)** Put the top back on the rice cooker and dial it up to the normal rice setting. **(4)** After that, gently remove the cover and give everything a good swirl. **(5)** Hot is best.

146. ALOO GOBI

Total Time: 30 minutes | Prep Time: 15 minutes

Ingredients:

2 potatoes, peeled and diced

1 onion, chopped

2 cloves garlic, minced

1 teaspoon turmeric powder

Salt to taste

2 cups cauliflower florets

1 tomato, chopped

1 teaspoon cumin seeds

1 teaspoon garam masala

Directions:

(1) Get the rice cooker hot and set it to sauté. Split the cumin seeds and add them. **(2)** Sauté the onion and garlic until they are chopped. Cook until a golden brown color appears. **(3)** Chop some potatoes and throw in some florets of cauliflower. Mix thoroughly. **(4)** Season with salt, turmeric powder, garam masala, and diced tomato. Thoroughly combine. **(5)** Put the top back on the rice cooker and dial it up to the normal rice setting. **(6)** After that, find out whether the cauliflower and potatoes are soft by opening the lid. **(7)** Hot is best.

147. FISH CHOPS

Total Time: 25 minutes | Prep Time: 10 minutes

Ingredients:

4 fish fillets (any white fish), cut into chunks

1 onion, finely chopped

2 tablespoons breadcrumbs

1 teaspoon lemon juice

Salt and pepper to taste

1 egg, beaten

1 teaspoon paprika

Directions:

(1) Combine the fish, chopped onion, breadcrumbs, vinegar, salt, pepper, paprika, and beaten egg in a bowl. (2) Pat or cut the mixture into tiny pieces. (3) Carefully arrange the fish chops in the rice cooker pot so they do not overlap. (4) Put the top back on the rice cooker and dial it up to the normal rice setting. (5) When it's done, test the fish for doneness by gently opening the lid. (6) Top with your preferred dipping sauce and serve hot.

148.   CHICKEN PIZZAIOLA

Total Time: 30 minutes | Prep Time: 10 minutes

Ingredients:

4 boneless, skinless chicken breasts

1 bell pepper, sliced

1 cup shredded mozzarella cheese

Salt and pepper to taste

1 cup marinara sauce

1 onion, sliced

1 teaspoon dried basil

Directions:

(1) Pepper and salt the chicken breasts. (2) Reduce heat to low and add marinara sauce to the rice cooker. (3) Before adding the sauce, season the chicken breasts. (4) Slicing the bell pepper and onion, arrange them over the chicken. (5) Finish with a sprinkle of dried basil and shredded mozzarella cheese. (6) Put the top back on the rice cooker and dial it up to the normal rice setting. (7) After that, check the chicken for doneness and cheese melting by gently opening the cover. Hot is best.

149.   VEGETABLE FRIED RICE

Total Time: 30 minutes | Prep Time: 10 minutes

Ingredients:

2 cups cooked rice

2 eggs, beaten

2 tablespoons vegetable oil

Salt and pepper to taste

1 cup mixed vegetables (carrots, peas, corn)

2 tablespoons soy sauce

2 cloves garlic, minced

Directions:

(1) In the rice cooker, heat the vegetable oil in sauté mode. (2) Sauté the minced garlic until it releases its aroma. (3) After a few minutes of stirring, add the mixed veggies. (4) Remove the veggies from the stove & add the beaten eggs to the rice cooker. Beat the eggs until they're fully done. (5) Include the soy sauce and cooked rice. Mix thoroughly. (6) Taste & add salt & pepper as needed. (7) Recover the rice cooker and continue cooking for an additional 5 minutes. (8) Warm up and savor!

150.   BEEF STEW

Total Time: 30 minutes | Prep Time: 10 minutes

Ingredients:

1 lb beef stew meat,

2 potatoes, diced

cubed

1 onion, chopped

2 carrots, sliced

2 cups beef broth

2 tablespoons

1 teaspoon Worcestershire sauce	tomato paste Salt and pepper to taste

Directions:

(1) Before cooking, season the beef stew with salt and pepper. *(2)* Put the carrots, onion, potatoes, and beef stew meat in the rice cooker. *(3)* Get a second bowl and combine the Worcestershire sauce, tomato paste, and beef broth. Once the rice cooker is ready, pour the ingredients over it. *(4)* After 20 minutes of sealing the rice cooker, switch it to the stew/soup setting. *(5)* After finishing, set aside for a few minutes to rest before serving. *(6)* Enjoy this easy beef stew while it's hot!

151. WALDORF SALAD

Total Time: 20 minutes | Prep Time: 10 minutes

Ingredients:

2 apples, diced	1 cup celery, chopped
1/2 cup walnuts, chopped	1/4 cup raisins
1/2 cup mayonnaise	1 tablespoon lemon juice
Salt and pepper to taste	

Directions:

(1) Get a bowl and toss in some chopped celery, walnuts, raisins, and diced apples. *(2)* Combine the mayonnaise, lemon juice, salt, and pepper in a separate small bowl and whisk to combine. *(3)* Toss the salad ingredients with the dressing until thoroughly combined. *(4)* Take a bite of your Waldorf Salad and enjoy it cold!

152. CHICKEN POMODORO

Total Time: 30 minutes | Prep Time: 10 minutes

Ingredients:

4 boneless, skinless chicken breasts	2 cups cherry tomatoes, halved
2 cloves garlic, minced	1/4 cup fresh basil, chopped
2 tablespoons olive oil	Salt and pepper to taste

Directions:

(1) Pepper and salt the chicken breasts. *(2)* While the rice cooker is on the sauté setting, heat the olive oil. *(3)* Sauté the minced garlic until it releases its aroma. *(4)* Brown the chicken breasts in a skillet over middle heat, stirring occasionally, for 3 to 4 minutes on each side. *(5)* While the rice is cooking, throw in some chopped basil and cherry tomatoes. *(6)* Once the chicken is done, cover the rice cooker and put it on stew/soup mode for 15 minutes. *(7)* After finishing, set aside for a few minutes to rest before serving. *(8)* This easy Chicken Pomodoro is best served hot.

153. GARLIC BUTTER SHRIMP

Total Time: 25 minutes | Prep Time: 10 minutes

Ingredients:

1 pound of large shrimp, peeled	3 tablespoons of butter
4 cloves of garlic, minced	1 tablespoon of lemon juice
Salt and pepper to taste	Chopped parsley for garnish

Directions:

(1) The shrimp should be rinsed with cold water and dried with paper towels. *(2)* Set the

rice cooker to sauté mode and melt the butter. *(3)* Bring the minced garlic to a fragrant simmer approximately 1 minute later. *(4)* Once the rice cooker is hot, add the shrimp and simmer for three to four minutes or until they begin to turn pink. *(5)* Toss in the pepper, salt, and lemon juice. *(6)* Hot shrimp, topped with minced parsley, served immediately.

154.   CHICKEN MILANESE

Total Time: 30 minutes | Prep Time: 15 minutes

Ingredients:

2 boneless, skinless chicken breasts	1 cup of breadcrumbs
1/2 cup of grated Parmesan cheese	2 eggs, beaten
Salt and pepper to taste	Olive oil for frying

Directions:

(1) Flatten the chicken breasts using a mallet. *(2)* Combine the breadcrumbs and Parmesan on a shallow plate. *(3)* Mix the pepper and salt into the chicken breasts. *(4)* Coat each chicken breast with the breadcrumb mixture after dipping it in beaten eggs. *(5)* Set the rice cooker to sauté mode and add olive oil to heat it up. *(6)* After adding the chicken breasts to the rice cooker, simmer for 5 to 6 minutes on each side or until browned and done. *(7)* Hot chicken Milanese served with a side of your choice.

155.   TARAMOSALATA

Total Time: 20 minutes | Prep Time: 10 minutes

Ingredients:

200g tarama (fish roe)	1 small onion, grated
1/4 cup lemon juice	1/2 cup olive oil
2 slices of white bread, crust removed	Water

Directions:

(1) Allow the bread slices to soak in water for a few minutes before squeezing out any extra moisture. *(2)* Add the soaked bread, grated onion, lemon juice, and tarama to a food processor. Mix until combined. *(3)* Slowly drizzle olive oil into the food processor while it is running until a creamy mixture forms. *(4)* Chill the taramosalata until it's time to serve by transferring it to a serving platter. *(5)* With pita bread or crackers, serve the taramosalata cold.

156.   DAL MAKHANI

Total Time: 30 minutes | Prep Time: 10 minutes

Ingredients:

1 cup black lentils (whole urad dal), rinsed and soaked overnight	1/4 cup red kidney beans (rajma), rinsed and soaked overnight
1 onion, finely chopped	2 tomatoes, pureed
2 cloves garlic, minced	1-inch ginger, grated
1 teaspoon cumin seeds	1 teaspoon garam masala
1/2 teaspoon turmeric	Salt to taste

powder

2 tablespoons butter	1/4 cup cream

Directions:

(1) After the lentils and kidney beans have soaked, drain them and give them another rinse. *(2)* Sauté the butter and cumin seeds in a rice cooker set to the sauté setting. Ignore their spluttering. *(3)* Chopped garlic, ginger, and onions should be added. Cook the onions in a skillet until they become pale and soft. *(4)* Garam masala, salt, turmeric powder, and

pureed tomatoes should be added. Soften the tomatoes by cooking them. *(5)* Combine 4 cups of water with the kidney beans and lentils that have been rinsed. Mix thoroughly. *(6)* Ten minutes should be enough time to cook the rice under pressure in a rice cooker. *(7)* Carefully open the lid after manually releasing the pressure. *(8)* Before adding the cream, taste and season to taste. *(9)* Top with naan or rice and serve hot.

157. SHEPHERD'S PIE

Total Time: 30 minutes | Prep Time: 10 minutes

Ingredients:

1 pound ground beef	1 onion, diced
2 cloves garlic, minced	1 cup frozen mixed vegetables
1 cup beef broth	2 tablespoons tomato paste
Salt and pepper, to taste	2 cups mashed potatoes
1 cup shredded cheddar cheese	

Directions:

(1) Brown the ground beef in the rice cooker on sauté mode. Saute the minced garlic & chopped onion until they soften. *(2)* Beef broth, tomato paste, and frozen mixed veggies should be stirred in. Add a little salt & pepper to taste. Put the cover on and turn the stovetop on low to cook the rice. *(3)* Just a little thickening should be achieved after 10 to fifteen minutes of cooking. *(4)* After the filling is finished, top with mashed potatoes. On top, crumble some cheddar cheese. *(5)* Keep the cover on and simmer for another 5 to 10 minutes or until the potatoes are warm and the cheese has melted. *(6)* Warm up and savor!

158. BUTTER CHICKEN

Total Time: 30 minutes | Prep Time: 10 minutes

Ingredients:

1 pound boneless, skinless chicken breasts	1 onion, finely chopped
2 cloves garlic, minced	1 tablespoon butter
1 cup tomato puree	1/2 cup heavy cream
1 tablespoon garam masala	1 teaspoon ground turmeric
Salt and pepper, to taste	Fresh cilantro for garnish

Directions:

(1) To soften the onions and garlic, melt the butter and sauté them in the rice cooker on sauté mode. *(2)* Once the chicken is no longer pink, add the pieces and continue cooking. *(3)* Be sure to include tomato puree, heavy cream, garam masala, turmeric, salt, and pepper. Put the cover on and turn the stovetop on low to cook the rice. *(4)* After the chicken is done and the sauce has thickened, continue cooking for another 10 to 15 minutes . *(5)* Before serving, top with chopped fresh cilantro. Pair with steamed rice and naan bread.

159. BEEF TACOS

Total Time: 25 minutes | Prep Time: 10 minutes

Ingredients:

1 pound ground beef	1 packet of taco seasoning
1/2 cup water	8 taco shells
Shredded lettuce, diced tomatoes, shredded cheese, and	

sour cream for topping

(1) Brown the ground beef in the rice cooker on sauté mode. *(2)* After removing any leftover fat, combine the taco seasoning with water. Blend well by stirring. *(3)* Put the cover on and turn the stovetop on low to cook the rice. Stirring periodically; cook for 5 to 10 minutes or until a thick consistency is achieved. *(4)* Follow the package directions to reheat the taco shells while the meat cooks. *(5)* Spoon the meat mixture into each taco shell when it has cooked. Scatter chopped tomatoes, shredded cheese, sour cream, and lettuce on top. *(6)* Enjoy right away after serving!

160.   ALMOND CRUSTED SALMON

Total Time: 20 minutes | Prep Time: 10 minutes

Ingredients:

4 salmon fillets	Salt and pepper, to taste
1/2 cup almond meal	2 tablespoons Dijon mustard
1 tablespoon honey	Lemon wedges for serving

Directions:

(1) Add salt & pepper to the salmon fillets. *(2)* After coating each fillet with Dijon mustard, sprinkle with honey. *(3)* Press lightly to adhere, coating each fillet with almond meal. *(4)* Before you start cooking the rice, put the salmon fillets in the rice cooker and cover it. *(5)* Once the crust has become golden brown and the salmon is opaque throughout, heat for another 8 to 10 minutes . *(6)* Warm the dish and garnish with lemon wedges. *(7)* The almond-coated fish is easy to make and tastes great.

161.   SWEET AND SOUR CHICKEN

Total Time: 25 minutes | Prep Time: 10 minutes

Ingredients:

1 lb boneless, skinless chicken breasts, diced	1 bell pepper, diced
1 onion, diced	1 cup pineapple chunks
½ cup sweet and sour sauce	2 tablespoons vegetable oil
Salt and pepper to taste	

Directions:

(1) Place diced chicken, bell pepper, onion, and pineapple chunks into the rice cooker. *(2)* Pour sweet and sour sauce over the ingredients. *(3)* Season with salt and pepper. *(4)* Close the rice cooker lid and set it to cook for 15 minutes . *(5)* Once cooked, open the lid, stir the contents, and let it sit for a few minutes before serving. *(6)* Serve hot cooked rice.

162.   CHICKEN MALLOREDDUS

Total Time: 30 minutes | Prep Time: 10 minutes

Ingredients:

1 lb chicken thighs, diced

1 cup malloreddus pasta	2 cups chicken broth
1 onion, finely chopped	2 cloves garlic, minced
1 tablespoon olive oil	Salt and pepper to taste
Grated Parmesan cheese for garnish	Chopped fresh parsley for garnish

Directions:

(1) Warm the rice cooker's insert with olive oil.
(2) Sauté the chopped garlic and onion until they release their aroma. (3) Before they brown, add the diced chicken thighs. (4) Throw in the chicken broth and malloreddus pasta and mix well. (5) Add a little salt & pepper to taste. (6) After adding the rice to the cooker, cover it and cook it for 20 minutes . (7) To serve, remove the cover after cooking, mix the contents, and set it aside for a few minutes to rest. (8) Crumbled fresh parsley and grated Parmesan cheese make a nice garnish. Serve hot.

163.   CHICKEN STELLINE

Total Time: 30 minutes | Prep Time: 10 minutes

Ingredients:

1 lb chicken breast, diced	1 cup stelline pasta
2 cups chicken broth	1 carrot, diced
1 celery stalk, diced	1 onion, diced
2 cloves garlic, minced	1 tablespoon olive oil
Salt and pepper to taste	Chopped fresh parsley for garnish

Directions:

(1) Warm the rice cooker's insert with olive oil.
(2) Sauté the chopped garlic and onion until they release their aroma. (3) Before they brown, add the diced chicken thighs. (4) Throw in the chicken broth and malloreddus pasta and mix well. (5) Add a little salt & pepper to taste. (6) After adding the rice to the cooker, cover it and cook it for 20 minutes . (7) To serve, remove the cover after cooking, mix the contents, and set it aside for a few minutes to rest. (8) Crumbled fresh parsley and grated Parmesan cheese make a nice garnish. Serve hot.

164.   CHICKEN PARMESAN

Total Time: 30 minutes | Prep Time: 10 minutes

Ingredients:

1 lb chicken breasts, pounded thin	1 cup bread crumbs
1/2 cup grated Parmesan cheese	1 egg, beaten
1 cup marinara sauce	1 cup shredded mozzarella cheese
2 tablespoons olive oil	Salt and pepper to taste
Chopped fresh basil for garnish	

Directions:

(1) Combine the breadcrumbs and Parmesan cheese in a shallow dish. (2) Before coating with breadcrumb mixture, dip chicken breasts in beaten egg. (3) Warm the rice cooker's insert with olive oil. (4) Brown the coated chicken breasts in the rice cooker for about 5 minutes on each side. (5) Coat the chicken breasts with marinara sauce. (6) Shred some mozzarella cheese and sprinkle it on top. (7) Place the cover on top of the rice cooker & cook on high heat for 15 minutes. (8) Remove the chicken from the heat, top with chopped

fresh basil, and cover to keep it warm for a few minutes. Then, serve. *(9)* With cooked spaghetti or crusty bread, serve hot.

165.   CRAB ETOUFFEE

Total Time: 30 minutes | Prep Time: 10 minutes

Ingredients:

1 cup white rice	1 tablespoon olive oil
1 onion, diced	2 cloves garlic, minced
1 bell pepper, diced	1 celery stalk, diced
1 teaspoon Cajun seasoning	1 can diced tomatoes
1 cup chicken broth	1 pound lump crabmeat
Salt and pepper to taste	

Directions:

(1) After washing the rice in cold water, make sure the water is clear. *(2)* After you've measured out the water needed for the rice cooker, add the rice and follow the manufacturer's directions. *(3)* With the heat set to medium, warm the olive oil in a big skillet. *(4)* Be sure to include the celery, onion, garlic, and bell pepper. Just give it a quick 5-minute cook till it's mushy. *(5)* Add the chicken stock, diced tomatoes, and Cajun spice; stir to combine. Continue to simmer for another ten minutes . *(6)* Toss in the lump crabmeat gently and heat for about 5 minutes or until cooked thoroughly. *(7)* Taste & add salt & pepper as needed. Top the cooked rice with the crab etouffee.

166.   CEDAR PLANK SALMON

Total Time: 25 minutes | Prep Time: 5 minutes

Ingredients:

1 cup white rice	1 cedar plank
4 salmon fillets	2 tablespoons olive oil
Salt and pepper to taste	Lemon wedges for serving

Directions:

(1) After washing the rice in cold water, make sure the water is clear. After you've measured out the water needed for the rice cooker, add the rice and follow the manufacturer's directions. *(2)* Ten minutes is the minimum amount of time to soak the cedar plank in water. *(3)* The rice cooker should be preheated to steam. *(4)* After seasoning the salmon fillets with salt and pepper, rub them with olive oil. *(5)* Arrange the salmon fillets on the cedar board before placing them in the rice cooker. *(6)* After the salmon has cooked for about 15 minutes, cover the rice cooker and continue cooking. *(7)* With lemon wedges, serve the cedar plank salmon.

167.   SPINACH AND ARTICHOKE DIP

Total Time: 30 minutes | Prep Time: 10 minutes

Ingredients:

1 cup white rice	1 package of frozen chopped spinach, thawed & drained
1 can artichoke hearts, drained	1 cup grated Parmesan cheese
1 cup mayonnaise	1 cup sour cream
1 teaspoon garlic powder	Salt and pepper to taste

Directions:

(1) After washing the rice in cold water, make sure the water is clear. After you've measured out the water needed for the rice cooker, add the rice and follow the manufacturer's

directions. *(2)* Put the chopped artichoke hearts, spinach, Parmesan, mayonnaise, sour cream & garlic powder in a bowl and mix well. Combine thoroughly. *(3)* Taste and add salt & pepper as needed. *(4)* Place the rice cooker inside a heatproof dish and transfer the ingredients to it. *(5)* After around 15 minutes of cooking, cover the rice cooker and let the dip bubble and get hot. *(6)* Dip the bread or tortilla chips in the spinach and artichoke mixture and serve.

168.   CHICKEN TRENNE

Total Time: 30 minutes | Prep Time: 10 minutes

Ingredients:

1 cup white rice	1 tablespoon olive oil
1 pound chicken breast	1 onion, diced
2 cloves garlic, minced	1 teaspoon Italian seasoning
1 (1*(4)*5 oz) can diced tomatoes	1 cup chicken broth
8 oz tonne pasta	Salt and pepper to taste

Directions:

(1) After washing the rice in cold water, make sure the water is clear. After you've measured out the water needed for the rice cooker, add the rice and follow the manufacturer's directions. *(2)* With the heat set to medium, warm the olive oil in a big skillet. After about 5 minutes , add the chicken breasts and heat until they are browned on both sides. *(3)* Toss in the minced garlic and chopped onion and sauté for about three minutes, or until the vegetables are tender. *(4)* Combine the trenne pasta with the chicken stock, diced tomatoes, Italian spice, and a good stir. Simmer for about 10 minutes or until the pasta reaches an al dente texture. *(5)* Taste & add salt & pepper as needed. *(6)* With the prepared rice served on the side, serve the chicken trenne hot.

169.   CHICKEN SCAMPI

Total Time: 30 minutes | Prep Time: 10 minutes

Ingredients:

1 lb chicken breast, diced	8 oz linguine pasta
3 cloves garlic, minced	1/4 cup butter
1/4 cup white wine	1/4 cup chicken broth
1/4 cup lemon juice	Salt and pepper to taste
Fresh parsley for garnish	

Directions:

(1) Use the rice cooker to cook the linguine pasta as directed on the box. *(2)* Melt the butter over middle heat in a saucepan while the pasta cooks. Sauté the minced garlic until it releases its aroma. *(3)* Cook the diced chicken until it is browned and cooked through in the skillet. *(4)* Mix in the chicken broth, white wine, and lemon juice. Keep the sauce simmering for 5 minutes or until it thickens just a little. *(5)* Drain the pasta & toss it with the chicken & sauce in the pan after it's done. Toss lightly to coat. *(6)* After you taste it, add salt and pepper and top it off with some fresh parsley.

170.   FETTUCCINE ALFREDO

Total Time: 25 minutes | Prep Time: 5 minutes

Ingredients:

8 oz fettuccine pasta	1/2 cup heavy cream
1/4 cup grated Parmesan cheese	2 tbsp butter
Salt and pepper to taste	Fresh parsley for garnish

Directions:

(1) In a rice cooker, prepare the fettuccine pasta according to the package directions. *(2)* Melt the butter in a skillet over middle heat with the heavy cream. *(3)* Once the sauce has thickened and smoothed out, stir in the grated Parmesan. *(4)* After the pasta is done cooking, rinse it and toss it with the Alfredo sauce in the pot. Toss lightly to coat. *(5)* After you taste it, add salt & pepper and top it off with some fresh parsley.

171.   CHICKEN PRIMAVERA

Total Time: 30 minutes | Prep Time: 15 minutes

Ingredients:

1 lb chicken breast, sliced	8 oz penne pasta
1 cup broccoli florets	1/2 cup sliced carrots
1/2 cup sliced bell peppers	1/4 cup chicken broth
1/4 cup heavy cream	2 tbsp olive oil
Salt and pepper to taste	Grated Parmesan cheese for garnish

Directions:

(1) Add broccoli florets & sliced carrots to the rice cooker with the penne pasta in the final five minutes of cooking, following the package directions. *(2)* Get the olive oil going in a pan over middle heat while the pasta is cooking. Toss in the sliced chicken and cook it until it's browned and done. *(3)* Sauté the sliced bell peppers in the pan until they are soft. *(4)* Add the heavy cream and chicken broth. Keep the sauce simmering for 5 minutes or until it thickens just a little. *(5)* After the pasta and veggies are done cooking, drain them and include them in the pan with the chicken and sauce. Toss lightly to coat. *(6)* Toss with freshly ground pepper and salt, then top with grated Parmesan   cheese.

172.   MOUSSAKA

Total Time: 30 minutes | Prep Time: 15 minutes

Ingredients:

1 lb ground lamb or beef	2 medium eggplants, sliced
1 cup chopped onion	2 cloves garlic, minced
1 can diced tomatoes	1/4 cup tomato paste
1/2 cup grated Parmesan cheese	1/4 cup breadcrumbs
2 tbsp olive oil	Salt and pepper to taste
Fresh parsley for garnish	

Directions:

(1) Get the rice cooker hot by using the sauté setting. Season with chopped onion, minced garlic, and olive oil. Cook until tender. *(2)* Brown the ground meat in the rice cooker, whether it's lamb or beef. *(3)* Toss in the tomato paste, chopped tomatoes, salt, and pepper. Once the flavors have blended, cook for another 5 minutes . *(4)* Prior to incorporating the meat mixture into the rice cooker, arrange eggplant slices on top. *(5)*

Grated Parmesan and breadcrumbs should be mixed in a small basin. On top of the eggplant layer, sprinkle equally. *(6)* Put the cover back on the rice cooker and turn it on to cook rice.

To make the eggplant soft and the topping golden brown, cook for around ten to fifteen minutes. *(7)* Prior to serving, top with chopped fresh parsley.

173.   BEEF WELLINGTON

Total Time: 30 minutes | Prep Time: 10 minutes

Ingredients:

4 beef fillets	Salt and pepper to taste
1 tablespoon olive oil	4 slices of prosciutto
4 tablespoons mushroom duxelles	1 sheet puff pastry, thawed
1 egg, beaten (for egg wash)	

Directions:

(1) Dress the meat fillets with pepper and salt. *(2)* While the rice cooker is on the sauté setting, heat the olive oil. *(3)* The fillets should be seared for about two minutes on each side or until they brown. *(4)* While the fillets are cooling, remove them from the pan. *(5)* Scatter a piece of prosciutto around each fillet. *(6)* On top of the prosciutto, spread the mushroom duxelles. *(7)* Puff pastry should be rolled out and cut into pieces that are big enough to encase each fillet. *(8)* Seal the edges of the puff pastry & wrap each fillet in it. *(9)* Coat the dough with an egg wash. *(10)* Put the fillets in the rice cooker and cook them for 20 minutes with the wrappers still on. *(11)* Serve right away when finished.

174.   CHICKEN CENCIONI

Total Time: 30 minutes | Prep Time: 10 minutes

Ingredients:

4 chicken breasts	Salt and pepper to taste
2 tablespoons olive oil	1 cup cherry tomatoes, halved
4 cloves garlic, minced	1 tablespoon Italian seasoning
1/4 cup white wine	1/4 cup chicken broth
2 tablespoons chopped fresh basil	

Directions:

(1) Rub some Italian seasoning, salt & pepper onto the chicken breasts. *(2)* While the rice cooker is on the sauté setting, heat the olive oil. *(3)* Brown the chicken breasts in a skillet over middle heat for approximately 3 minutes on each side. *(4)* Cook the cherry tomatoes and garlic for 2 minutes in the cooker. *(5)* While stirring, pour in the chicken broth & white wine. *(6)* Put the rice cooker on high heat for 15 minutes with the lid closed. *(7)* After that, top with chopped fresh basil and serve while still hot.

175.   SPAGHETTI BOLOGNESE

Total Time: 30 minutes | Prep Time: 10 minutes

Ingredients:

8 ounces spaghetti	1 tablespoon olive oil
1 onion, finely	2 cloves garlic, minced
chopped	
1 pound ground beef	Salt and pepper to taste
1 can (14 ounces)	1 teaspoon dried

crushed tomatoes

1/2 teaspoon dried basil

oregano

Grated Parmesan cheese for garnish

Directions:

(1) After cooking the spaghetti as directed on the box, drain it and put it aside. **(2)** While the rice cooker is on the sauté setting, heat the olive oil. **(3)** Chop the garlic and onion and sauté them until they are tender. **(4)** Brown the ground beef by adding it to the pan after seasoning it with salt and pepper. **(5)** Add the oregano, basil, and smashed tomatoes and mix well. **(6)** Put the rice cooker on high heat for 10 minutes with the lid closed. **(7)** Add cooked spaghetti and top with Parmesan cheese when done.

176.   LEMON DILL SALMON

Total Time: 25 minutes | Prep Time: 10 minutes

Ingredients:

4 salmon fillets	Salt and pepper to taste
2 tablespoons olive oil	Zest and juice of 1 lemon
2 tablespoons chopped fresh dill	

Directions:

(1) Add salt, pepper, lemon zest, and minced dill to the salmon fillets. **(2)** While the rice cooker is on the sauté setting, heat the olive oil. **(3)** If you want crispy salmon fillets, skin side down and fry them for around three minutes . **(4)** Cook the salmon fillets for a further 2 minutes after flipping them. **(5)** Pour the fillets with the squeezed lemon juice. **(6)** Put the rice cooker on high heat for 10 minutes with the lid closed. **(7)** Serve immediately with your preferred accompaniments.

177.   PHILLY CHEESESTEAK

Total Time: 30 minutes | Prep Time: 10 minutes

Ingredients:

1 pound thinly sliced beef sirloin	1 onion, thinly sliced
1 green bell pepper, thinly sliced	4 slices provolone cheese
Salt and pepper to taste	Hoagie rolls

Directions:

(1) Add salt and pepper to the beef sirloin. **(2)** Before adding the rice to the cooker, brown the meat with the onion and pepper. **(3)** After 20 minutes of cooking, cover the rice cooker and remove the lid. **(4)** After it is done, spoon the mixture into the hoagie buns and top with a provolone cheese slice for each. **(5)** Roll up the hoagies and enjoy while they're hot.

178.   COLESLAW

Total Time: 15 minutes | Prep Time: 15 minutes

Ingredients:

4 cups shredded cabbage	1 carrot, grated
1/2 cup mayonnaise	2 tablespoons apple cider vinegar
1 tablespoon honey	Salt and pepper to taste

Directions:

(1) Mix mayonnaise, honey, apple cider vinegar, salt & pepper in a mixing bowl. Whisk to combine. *(2)* Put grated carrots and shredded cabbage into the rice cooker. *(3)* Toss the veggies with the dressing and mix until evenly coated. *(4)* Put the rice cooker on high heat for 15 minutes with the lid closed. *(5)* Before serving as a side, give it one last toss.

179. BBQ CHICKEN

Total Time: 30 minutes | Prep Time: 10 minutes

Ingredients:

4 boneless, skinless chicken breasts	1 cup BBQ sauce
2 tablespoons olive oil	Salt and pepper to taste

Directions:

(1) Mix the pepper and salt into the chicken breasts. *(2)* Brown the chicken breasts on all sides by searing them in olive oil in a pan over medium-high heat. *(3)* Marinade the chicken breasts in the barbecue sauce and then place them in the rice cooker. *(4)* After 20 minutes of cooking, cover the rice cooker and remove the lid. *(5)* After it's done, cut the chicken into slices and top with more BBQ sauce if you want.

180. CHICKEN ORECCHIETTE

Total Time: 30 minutes | Prep Time: 10 minutes

Ingredients:

8 ounces orecchiette pasta	2 boneless, skinless chicken breasts, diced
1 cup chicken broth	1/2 cup heavy cream
1 cup broccoli florets	1/4 cup grated Parmesan cheese
Salt and pepper to taste	

Directions:

(1) In a rice cooker, combine orecchiette pasta, minced chicken breasts, chicken broth, heavy cream, broccoli florets, salt, and pepper. *(2)* After 20 minutes of cooking, cover the rice cooker and remove the lid. *(3)* When finished, carefully incorporate the grated Parmesan cheese by stirring until melted. *(4)* Warm the dish before serving and top with more Parmesan cheese, if preferred.

181. SOUTHERN FRIED CHICKEN

Total Time: 30 minutes | Prep Time: 15 minutes

Ingredients:

4 chicken thighs, bone-in	1 cup all-purpose flour
1 teaspoon salt	1 teaspoon black pepper
1 teaspoon paprika	1 teaspoon garlic powder
1 teaspoon onion powder	Vegetable oil for frying

Directions:

(1) Combine the flour, pepper, salt, paprika, garlic powder, and onion powder in a shallow dish. *(2)* Scatter the flour mixture over each chicken thigh, being sure to shake off any excess. *(3)* Before you put the rice cooker on high heat, make sure it's covered with vegetable oil. *(4)* Put the chicken thighs in the heated oil, skin side down, and cook until done. *(5)* Flip halfway through cooking time for ten to twelve minutes or until crisp and

golden brown. *(6)* After removing the chicken from the rice cooker, place it on a paper towel-lined plate to drain. Once drained, serve.

182.   SHRIMP SCAMPI

Total Time: 25 minutes | Prep Time: 10 minutes

Ingredients:

1 pound shrimp, peeled and deveined
2 tablespoons butter
1/4 cup white wine

Salt and pepper to taste

4 cloves garlic, minced
2 tablespoons olive oil
1/4 cup fresh lemon juice
Chopped parsley for garnish

Directions:

(1) While the rice cooker is on the sauté setting, melt the butter and olive oil. *(2)* Garlic, when minced, should be sautéed for one or two minutes to release its aroma. *(3)* Toss in the shrimp and cook for two or three minutes or until opaque and pink. *(4)* Add the white wine & lemon juice, then add the salt & pepper & mix everything together. *(5)* Keep cooking for another two or three minutes or until the sauce starts to thicken a little. *(6)* Add some chopped parsley as a garnish just before serving.

183.   CHICKEN FAJITAS

Total Time: 30 minutes | Prep Time: 15 minutes

Ingredients:

1 pound chicken breasts, thinly sliced
1 bell pepper, sliced

2 tablespoons olive oil
Optional toppings: sour cream, salsa, shredded cheese, guacamole

1 onion, sliced

2 tablespoons fajita seasoning
Flour tortillas

Directions:

(1) Put the olive oil into the rice cooker and turn it to the sauté setting. *(2)* Sauté the chicken breasts until they are browned, then add the cut breasts. *(3)* Before stirring, add the bell pepper and onion slices to the saucepan along with the fajita spice. *(4)* Keep cooking for another 5 to 7 minutes or until chicken is done and veggies are soft. *(5)* Top chicken fajitas with your choice of toppings and serve over warm flour tortillas.

184.   BEEF STROGANOFF

Total Time: 30 minutes | Prep Time: 10 minutes

Ingredients:

1 pound beef sirloin, thinly sliced
8 ounces mushrooms, sliced
1 cup beef broth
2 tablespoons flour
Salt and pepper to

1 onion, chopped

2 cloves garlic, minced
1 cup sour cream
2 tablespoons butter
Cooked egg noodles

taste   or rice for serving

Directions:

(1) Put the rice cooker on sauté and melt the butter. *(2)* Saute the minced garlic & chopped onion until they soften. *(3)* Toss in the mushrooms and cut beef sirloin; sear the meat until it becomes brown. *(4)* To coat the meat

mixture, sprinkle flour on top and stir well. *(5)* Add the beef broth & whisk until it thickens. *(6)* After you've mixed the sour cream well, turn off the sauté setting. *(7)* Taste & add salt & pepper as needed. *(8)* Pile cooked egg noodles or rice on top of beef stroganoff.

185.   CHICKEN TRIA

Total Time: 30 minutes | Prep Time: 10 minutes

Ingredients:

2 boneless, skinless chicken breasts, diced	1 cup long-grain rice
1 ¾ cups chicken broth	1 tablespoon olive oil
1 small onion, finely chopped	2 cloves garlic, minced
1 teaspoon dried oregano	Salt and pepper to taste
1 lemon, sliced	Fresh parsley for garnish

Directions:

(1) After rinsing the rice under cold water until it runs clear, be sure to let it drain well. *(2)* In a rice cooker, heat the olive oil by turning it on to sauté mode. Before adding the chopped chicken, brown it for about three to four minutes . *(3)* Toss in the rice cooker with the minced garlic and chopped onion and cook for an additional 2 minutes or until aromatic. *(4)* Blend in the rice, chicken stock, dried oregano, pepper, salt, and salt. *(5)* Once you've selected white rice as your cooking method, cover the rice cooker and cook until the warm setting comes on. *(6)* After that, remove the cover and use a fork to fluff the rice. Garnish with fresh parsley & lemon slices, & serve hot.

186.   LAMB CHOPS

Total Time: 30 minutes | Prep Time: 5 minutes

Ingredients:

4 lamb chops	1 cup basmati rice
1 ¾ cups water	1 tablespoon olive oil
2 teaspoons dried rosemary	Salt and pepper to taste
Lemon wedges for serving	

Directions:

(1) Grind some dried rosemary into the lamb chops and season them with salt and pepper. *(2)* After rinsing it with cold water until it is clear, let the basmati rice drain well. *(3)* Next, combine the washed rice with the water and olive oil in the rice cooker. On top of the rice, arrange the lamb chops that have been seasoned. *(4)* Once you've selected white rice as your cooking method, cover the rice cooker and cook until the warm setting comes on. *(5)* After cooking is complete, set aside for a few minutes to rest. Warm the dish and garnish with lemon wedges.

187.   HUMMUS

Total Time: 15 minutes | Prep Time: 10 minutes

Ingredients:

1 can chickpeas,	2 cloves garlic,
drained	minced
3 tablespoons tahini	3 tablespoons lemon juice

2 tablespoons olive oil

½ teaspoon ground cumin

Salt to taste

Water, as needed

Paprika and olive oil for garnish

Directions:

(1) Grind the cumin seeds, add the salt, olive oil, lemon juice, tahini, and chopped garlic, and mix or process until smooth. *(2)* Add water to the blender as required to get the desired consistency & blend until smooth. *(3)* Before serving, spoon the hummus into a bowl, top with olive oil, and garnish with paprika. *(4)* For dipping, try pita bread, veggies, or crackers.

188. CHICKEN GORGONZOLA

Total Time: 30 minutes | Prep Time: 10 minutes

Ingredients:

2 boneless, skinless chicken breasts

1 cup arborio rice

1 ¾ cups chicken broth

¼ cup crumbled gorgonzola cheese

2 tablespoons butter

Salt and pepper to taste

Fresh parsley for garnish

Directions:

(1) After rinsing it with cold water until it is clear, let the arborio rice drain well. *(2)* Mix the pepper and salt into the chicken breasts. *(3)* Chop some chicken broth and put some butter in the rice cooker with the washed rice. On top of the rice, arrange the chicken breasts that have been seasoned. *(4)* Once you've selected white rice as your cooking method, cover the rice cooker and cook until the warm setting comes on. *(5)* Take the chicken breasts out of the rice cooker when they're done and cut them into strips. *(6)* To make a creamy sauce, melt the crumbled gorgonzola and stir it into the cooked rice. *(7)* A sprinkle of fresh parsley and some sliced chicken will top the gorgonzola rice. Have a nice dinner!

189. LOADED NACHOS

Total Time: 25 minutes | Prep Time: 10 minutes

Ingredients:

1 bag of tortilla chips

1 cup shredded cheese (cheddar or Mexican blend)

1 cup cooked black beans

1 cup diced tomatoes

1/2 cup sliced black olives

1/4 cup diced jalapeños

1/4 cup diced red onion

1/4 cup chopped cilantro

1 avocado, diced

Sour cream for serving

Salsa, for serving

Directions:

(1) Set the "Cook" setting on your rice cooker to start cooking. *(2)* In the rice cooker's base, arrange half of the tortilla chips. *(3)* Before topping the chips with half of the cheese, divide the black beans, tomatoes, olives, jalapeños, and red onion among the two halves. *(4)* Layer the remaining ingredients in the same way. *(5)* To make sure the cheese melts and bubbles, cover the rice cooker and simmer for 15 minutes . *(6)* Place the nachos with the fillings on a serving plate with care. *(7)* Serve topped with chopped cilantro and cubed avocado. *(8)* Top with salsa & sour cream, & serve hot.

190.   BEEF VINDALOO

Total Time: 30 minutes | Prep Time: 10 minutes

Ingredients:

1 pound beef, thinly sliced

1 onion, diced

1 teaspoon ginger, grated

1/2 cup coconut milk

Cooked rice for serving

2 tablespoons vindaloo paste

2 cloves garlic, minced

1 cup diced tomatoes

Salt and pepper, to taste

Naan bread for serving

Directions:

(1) Put the meat, vindaloo paste, ginger, onion, garlic, chopped tomatoes, and coconut milk into the rice cooker. *(2)* Taste & add salt & pepper as needed. *(3)* After adding the rice, cover the cooker and cook for 20 minutes using the "Cook" option. *(4)* Wait 5 minutes after finishing before opening the lid. *(5)* Mix the meat vindaloo well. *(6)* Overcooked rice, served hot with naan bread as a side.

191.   PALAK PANEER

Total Time: 30 minutes | Prep Time: 10 minutes

Ingredients:

1 block (14 ounces) paneer, cubed

1 onion, finely chopped

1 teaspoon ginger, grated

1/2 cup plain yogurt

Salt, to taste

2 tablespoons oil

2 cloves garlic, minced

2 cups spinach, chopped

1 teaspoon garam masala

Cooked rice or naan bread for serving

Directions:

(1) Put the rice cooker on the "Cook" option to heat up the oil. *(2)* Toss in the minced garlic, ginger, and onion. Cook the onions in a skillet until they become tender. *(3)* Toss in the paneer cubes and heat until they become a light golden brown. *(4)* Cook, stirring occasionally, until the chopped spinach wilts. *(5)* Combine the salt, garam masala, and yogurt in a small basin. *(6)* Add the yogurt mixture to the rice cooker and stir it. *(7)* After 10 minutes of cooking, cover and let cook. *(8)* After finishing, set aside for a few minutes to rest before serving. *(9)* Warm it up and serve it with some naan bread or boiled rice.

192.   CHICKEN CAPRESE

Total Time: 30 minutes | Prep Time: 10 minutes

Ingredients:

2 boneless, skinless chicken breasts

2 tablespoons olive oil

1 cup fresh basil leaves

Balsamic glaze for drizzling

Salt and pepper, to taste

2 tomatoes, sliced

8 ounces fresh mozzarella, sliced

Cooked pasta or crusty bread for

serving

Directions:

(1) Mix the pepper and salt into the chicken breasts. *(2)* While the rice cooker is on the "Cook" setting, heat the olive oil. *(3)* After a few minutes of cooking time, add the chicken breasts and continue cooking until they are fully cooked. *(4)* Take the chicken out of the

rice cooker after it's done cooking and put it aside. **(5)** In a rice cooker, layer the sliced mozzarella, fresh basil leaves, and sliced tomatoes. **(6)** After layering the rice cooker with tomato, basil, and mozzarella, add the chicken breasts again on top. **(7)** To melt the cheese, cover and simmer for another 5 minutes. **(8)** Top the chicken caprese with the balsamic glaze. **(9)** With cooked spaghetti or toasted bread, serve hot.

193. BEEF CHILI

Total Time: 30 minutes | Prep Time: 10 minutes

Ingredients:

1 lb ground beef	1 onion, diced
1 can diced tomatoes	1 can (15 oz) kidney beans, drained and rinsed
1 can (6 oz) tomato paste	1 cup beef broth
2 cloves garlic, minced	2 tbsp chili powder
1 tsp cumin	Salt and pepper to taste

Directions:

(1) Cook the ground beef, diced onions, and minced garlic in the rice cooker pot on "Sauté" mode until done. **(2)** Spice up your beef broth with chopped tomatoes, kidney beans, tomato paste, cumin, salt, and pepper. Mix thoroughly. **(3)** Put the rice cooker in "Cook" mode after you close the lid after 15 minutes of cooking, and strain. **(4)** After finishing, set aside for a few minutes to rest before serving. **(5)** For an extra touch, you may top it up with sour cream, chopped green onions, or shredded cheese.

194. JAMBALAYA

Total Time: 30 minutes | Prep Time: 10 minutes

Ingredients:

1 lb chicken breast, diced	1 lb smoked sausage, sliced
1 onion, diced	1 green bell pepper, diced
2 cloves garlic, minced	1 can tomatoes
1 cup chicken broth	1 cup long-grain white rice
2 tsp Cajun seasoning	Salt and pepper to taste

Directions:

(1) While the rice cooker is on "Sauté" mode, brown the diced chicken and sausage. **(2)** Chopped garlic, bell pepper, and onions should be added. Saute the veggies in oil until they're tender. **(3)** Add the rice, chicken broth, diced tomatoes, Cajun spice, salt, and pepper. Stir to combine. **(4)** Put the rice cooker in "Cook" mode after you close the lid. After 15 minutes of cooking, strain. **(5)** When cooked through, use a fork to fluff the rice before serving hot.

195. FALAFEL

Total Time: 30 minutes | Prep Time: 10 minutes

Ingredients:

1 can chickpeas, drained	1/4 cup chopped parsley	2 cloves garlic, minced	2 tbsp all-purpose flour
1/4 cup chopped cilantro	1 small onion, chopped	1 tsp ground cumin	1 tsp ground coriander
		Salt and pepper to taste	Vegetable oil for frying

(1) Put the chickpeas, parsley, cilantro, garlic, onion, flour, cumin, coriander, salt, and pepper into a food processor. Blend until the ingredients are gritty but still cohesive. *(2)* Roll or pat the mixture into little balls. *(3)* In a pan, warm the vegetable oil over middle heat. Flip the falafel over and fry for another three to four minutes or until crisp and golden brown. *(4)* Garnish with fresh veggies and serve hot with hummus, pita, or tahini sauce.

196.   BEEF ENCHILADAS

Total Time: 30 minutes | Prep Time: 10 minutes

Ingredients:

1 lb ground beef
1 can (10 oz) red enchilada sauce
1/4 cup chopped cilantro
Salt and pepper to taste

1 onion, diced
1 cup shredded cheddar cheese
8 small flour tortillas

Directions:

(1) When the rice cooker is on the "Sauté" setting, brown the ground meat and chopped onions. *(2)* Add half the enchilada sauce and stir to combine. Add salt and pepper to taste. *(3)* Set oven temperature to 350°F, or 175°C. *(4)* Roll up a tortilla with some of the beef mixtures spooned over it, then put it seam-side down in the rice cooker pot. *(5)* After the tortillas are rolled, pour the leftover enchilada sauce over them. *(6)* On top, crumble some cheddar cheese. *(7)* Put the rice cooker in "Cook" mode after you close the lid. After 15 minutes of cooking, the cheese should be melted and bubbling. *(8)* Drizzle chopped cilantro on top before guests are served.

197.   CHICKEN RIGATONI

Total Time: 30 minutes | Prep Time: 10 minutes

Ingredients:

250g rigatoni pasta

1 tablespoon olive oil
2 cloves garlic, minced

1 teaspoon dried oregano
Salt and pepper to taste
Fresh basil leaves for garnish (optional)

2 chicken breasts, diced
1 small onion, diced
1 can (400g) diced tomatoes
1 teaspoon dried basil
Grated Parmesan cheese for serving

Directions:

(1) To make sure the rigatoni is cooked al dente, follow the package directions. Rinse and reserve. *(2)* Olive oil should be heated in a big pan over medium heat while pasta is cooking. Chop some chicken and throw it in. Cook for 5-7 minutes or until it's browned and done. *(3)* Toss chopped garlic and onion with the chicken in the skillet. About 3 minutes into cooking, the onion should become transparent. *(4)* After adding the salt and pepper, mix in the diced tomatoes, dried oregano, and basil. Simmer gently for 5 minutes. *(5)* Before tossing in the cooked rigatoni, make sure the pasta is covered with the sauce. *(6)* Garnish with grated Parmesan and, if desired, fresh basil leaves just before serving.

198.   CAPRESE SALAD

Total Time: 15 minutes | Prep Time: 15 minutes

Ingredients:

2 large ripe   200g fresh mozzarella

tomatoes, sliced
Fresh basil leaves

Salt and pepper to
taste

cheese, sliced
2 tablespoons
balsamic glaze

(1) On a serving dish, alternate the layers of tomato and mozzarella slices. (2) Place a few sprigs of fresh basil between each slice of mozzarella and tomato. (3) The salad should be topped with balsamic glaze. (4) Taste & add salt & pepper as needed. (5) Quickly prepare and serve.

199.   CHICKEN FRANCESE

Total Time: 25 minutes | Prep Time: 10 minutes

Ingredients:

2 boneless, skinless
chicken breasts
1/2 cup all-purpose
flour
2 tablespoons olive oil
1/4 cup fresh lemon
juice
2 tablespoons
chopped fresh parsley

Salt and pepper to
taste
2 large eggs

1/2 cup chicken broth
2 tablespoons
unsalted butter

Directions:

(1) Pepper and salt the chicken breasts. (2) Shred the extra flour from the chicken before dredging it. (3) Whisk the eggs in a small bowl. Flour the chicken and then dip it into the beaten eggs. (4) In a big skillet, set it over medium-high to warm the olive oil. Cook the chicken for three to four minutes on each side or until it becomes golden brown and cooked through. Take the chicken out of the pan and put it aside. (5) Combine the chicken broth with the lemon juice in the same skillet. Reduce warm to low & simmer, stirring occasionally to scrape off any brown pieces from the pan. (6) Melt the butter and stir it into the sauce until it thickens slightly. (7) Throw the chicken back into the pan and coat it with the sauce. (8) Before serving, top with chopped parsley.

200.   BEEF CHOPS

Total Time: 30 minutes | Prep Time: 10 minutes

Ingredients:

4 beef chops (about
1 inch thick)
2 tablespoons olive
oil
1 teaspoon dried
thyme
1/2 cup beef broth

Salt and pepper to
taste
2 cloves garlic, minced

1 teaspoon dried
rosemary
2 tablespoons
Worcestershire sauce

Directions:

(1) Add salt and pepper to the meat chops. (2) In a big skillet, set it over medium-high to warm the olive oil. Brown the beef chops in a skillet over middle heat, stirring occasionally, for 3 to 4 minutes on each side. Take the steak chops out of the pan and put them aside. (3) Sauté the minced garlic with the dried thyme and rosemary in the same pan. After about one minute of cooking, the aroma should begin to waft through the pot. (4) Scrape the bottom of the pan for any browned pieces, then stir in the beef stock and Worcestershire sauce. (5) Put the steak chops back in the pan and cook them in the sauce until they reach the doneness you like, which should take around 7 to 10 minutes for medium-rare. (6) Warm the meat chops and spread the sauce over them.

201.   CHICKEN ROTELLE

Total Time: 30 minutes | Prep Time: 10 minutes

Ingredients:

1 cup rotelle pasta

1 cup diced tomatoes

1/4 cup grated Parmesan cheese

Salt and pepper to taste

1 boneless, skinless chicken breast, diced

1/2 cup chicken broth

1 teaspoon Italian seasoning

Directions:

(1) In the rice cooker, combine the rotelle pasta, chicken, tomatoes, chicken broth, Italian seasoning, salt, and pepper. *(2)* Mix everything together. *(3)* Press the "Quick Cook" or "White Rice" button on the rice cooker and then cover it. *(4)* Toss in the grated Parmesan cheese when the cycle is finished. *(5)* Warm up and savor!

202.   CHICKEN PAPPARDELLE

Total Time: 30 minutes | Prep Time: 10 minutes

Ingredients:

1 cup pappardelle pasta

1 cup sliced mushrooms

1/4 cup heavy cream

One tablespoon of olive oil

1 boneless, skinless chicken thigh, sliced

1/2 cup diced onions

1/4 cup chicken broth

Salt and pepper to taste

Directions:

(1) Toss in some olive oil and put the rice cooker on "Quick Cook" or "White Rice" mode. *(2)* Toss in the chopped onions, sliced mushrooms, and sliced chicken thighs once the oil is hot. *(3)* Cook the chicken & veggies in a skillet until they're soft. *(4)* Put the pappardelle pasta, chicken broth, heavy cream, salt, and pepper in the saucepan. *(5)* Mix everything together. *(6)* Turn the pasta periodically as it cooks under the cover until it reaches the desired doneness. *(7)* After that, serve while hot and savor!

203.   CHICKEN LASAGNA

Total Time: 30 minutes | Prep Time: 10 minutes

Ingredients:

3 lasagna noodles broken into smaller pieces

1 cup marinara sauce

1/4 cup ricotta cheese

Salt and pepper to taste

1 boneless, skinless chicken breast, diced

1 cup shredded mozzarella cheese

1 teaspoon dried basil

Directions:

(1) In a rice cooker saucepan, layer chopped chicken, shredded mozzarella and ricotta cheeses, crushed lasagna noodles, marinara sauce, salt, and pepper. *(2)* Keep adding layers until you've used all of the ingredients, finishing with cheese on top. *(3)* Press the "Quick Cook" or "White Rice" button on the rice cooker and then cover it. *(4)* After the cycle finishes, remove the cover and let it settle for a short period of time to solidify. *(5)* Warm up and savor!

204. LEMON HERB CHICKEN

Total Time: 30 minutes | Prep Time: 10 minutes

Ingredients:

1 boneless, skinless chicken breast	Zest and juice of 1 lemon
2 cloves garlic, minced	1 tablespoon chopped fresh herbs
1 tablespoon olive oil	Salt and pepper to taste

Directions:

(1) Combine the lemon zest, juice, garlic, olive oil, salt, and pepper in a small bowl. Add the chopped fresh herbs. *(2)* Before adding the chicken breasts to the rice cooker pot, coat them well with the lemon herb mixture. *(3)* Press the "Quick Cook" or "White Rice" button on the rice cooker and then cover it. *(4)* To ensure the chicken is fully cooked, open the cover once the cycle finishes. *(5)* Cook the chicken for a little longer, if necessary, to achieve doneness. *(6)* Warm up and savor!

205. CREAM OF BROCCOLI SOUP

Total Time: 30 minutes | Prep Time: 10 minutes

Ingredients:

2 cups chopped broccoli	1 small onion, finely chopped
2 cloves garlic, minced	3 cups vegetable or chicken broth
1 cup milk or cream	Salt and pepper to taste

Directions:

(1) Before adding liquid to the rice cooker, cut the onion & garlic & add the chopped broccoli. *(2)* Put the rice cooker in "Cook" mode and cover it for 20 minutes . *(3)* Carefully uncover the mixture and stir in the milk or cream when the timer goes off. *(4)* Pulsating the broth with an immersion blender or a conventional blender achieves a creamy consistency. *(5)* Taste & add salt & pepper as needed. *(6)* Warm up and savor!

206. LENTIL SOUP

Total Time: 30 minutes | Prep Time: 10 minutes

Ingredients:

1 cup dried lentils, rinsed	1 carrot, diced
1 celery stalk, diced	1 small onion, diced
2 cloves garlic, minced	4 cups vegetable or chicken broth
1 teaspoon ground cumin	Salt and pepper to taste

Directions:

(1) If using a rice cooker, add carrots, celery, onions, garlic, broth, and cumin. *(2)* After 25 minutes of cooking in the rice cooker, cover and turn it to the "Cook" setting. *(3)* Carefully remove the cover once the cooking cycle ends and give the soup a stir. *(4)* Taste & add salt & pepper as needed. *(5)* Warm up and savor!

207. CHICKEN SORRENTINO

Total Time: 30 minutes | Prep Time: 10 minutes

Ingredients:

2 boneless, skinless	1 cup marinara sauce

chicken breasts
1 cup shredded mozzarella cheese
1 teaspoon Italian seasoning

1/4 cup grated Parmesan cheese
Salt and pepper to taste

Directions:

(1) Add salt, pepper, and Italian seasoning to chicken breasts. *(2)* After preparing the rice, add the chicken breasts and marinara sauce to the cooker. *(3)* Put the rice cooker in "Cook" mode and cover it for 20 minutes . *(4)* After the chicken has finished cooking, top it with shredded mozzarella and grated Parmesan. *(5)* After a few minutes of closing the cover, the cheese should have melted. *(6)* Accompany it with a dish of veggies or pasta and serve hot.

208.   CHICKEN ROTINI

Total Time: 30 minutes | Prep Time: 10 minutes

Ingredients:

2 boneless, skinless chicken thighs, diced
2 cups chicken broth
1/2 cup chopped bell peppers
1 teaspoon Italian seasoning

2 cups rotini pasta

1 cup diced tomatoes
2 cloves garlic, minced
Salt and pepper to taste

Directions:

(1) Toss the rice cooker with the diced chicken thighs, rotini, chicken broth, tomatoes, peppers, garlic, and Italian seasoning. *(2)* Put the rice cooker in "Cook" mode and cover it for 20 minutes . *(3)* Carefully remove the cover when the cooking cycle ends, and toss the pasta and chicken to combine. *(4)* Taste & add salt & pepper as needed. *(5)* Warm up and savor!

209.   BEEF SHAWARMA

Total Time: 30 minutes | Prep Time: 10 minutes

Ingredients:

1 pound beef sirloin, thinly sliced
2 cloves garlic, minced
1 teaspoon paprika

Salt and pepper to taste
Juice of 1 lemon
Toppings: sliced tomatoes, cucumbers, onions, tahini sauce

2 tablespoons olive oil

1 teaspoon ground cumin
1 teaspoon ground coriander
1/4 cup plain yogurt

4 pita bread

Directions:

(1) Add the garlic, cumin, paprika, coriander, olive oil, salt, & pepper to a bowl & stir to combine. Before coating, add the meat slices. *(2)* In the rice cooker, add the seasoned meat. The steak should be cooked thoroughly after about fifteen to twenty minutes of cooking on the "Rice" or "Quick Cook" option. *(3)* In a small dish, combine the yogurt and lemon juice to create a sauce. Set aside while meat cooks. *(4)* After the meat is done cooking, place it on pita bread that has been warmed. Add sliced tomatoes, cucumbers, and onions on top. Drizzle some yogurt sauce on top.

210.   BUFFALO CHICKEN

Total Time: 25 minutes | Prep Time: 10 minutes

Ingredients:

1 pound chicken breast
2 tablespoons butter,

1/4 cup hot sauce
1 teaspoon garlic

melted
Salt and pepper to taste
Celery sticks and ranch dressing for serving

powder
1 cup cooked rice

After adding the chicken, toss it to coat. *(3)* Toss the chicken with the seasonings into the rice cooker. For about ten to fifteen minutes , or until the chicken is cooked through, use the "Quick Cook" or "Rice" mode. *(4)* Accompany the cooked rice with buffalo chicken, celery sticks, and ranch dressing.

Directions:

(1) Combine the garlic powder, spicy sauce, melted butter, salt, and pepper in a bowl. *(2)*

211.   STUFFED GRAPE LEAVES

Total Time: 30 minutes | Prep Time: 15 minutes

Ingredients:

1 jar grape leaves, drained
1/2 cup chopped fresh parsley
1/4 cup pine nuts
2 tablespoons lemon juice
Greek yogurt for serving

1 cup cooked rice

1/4 cup chopped fresh mint
2 tablespoons olive oil
Salt and pepper to taste

Directions:

Toss the cooked rice with the chopped parsley, mint, pine nuts, olive oil, lemon juice, salt, and pepper in a bowl. On top of each grape leaf, pour some rice mixture. Constrict the roll by rolling it up and tucking the edges in. In the rice cooker, place the grape leaves that have been filled. Warm through by cooking for about fifteen to twenty minutes on the "Rice" or "Quick Cook" option. Accompany the filled grape leaves with a dollop of Greek yogurt.

212.   CHICKEN MAFALDINE

Total Time: 30 minutes | Prep Time: 10 minutes

Ingredients:

8 ounces mafaldine pasta
1 onion, diced

1 cup chicken broth
1 teaspoon dried oregano
Grated Parmesan cheese for serving

1 pound chicken thighs, diced
2 cloves garlic, minced
1 cup marinara sauce
Salt and pepper to taste

Directions:

(1) What follows is a recipe for chicken broth, marinara sauce, mafaldine pasta, chopped chicken thighs, sliced onion, minced garlic, salt, pepper, and chicken broth. *(2)* Mix the ingredients together. Cook the pasta and chicken until they are cooked through, approximately 20-25 minutes , with the lid closed, on the "Quick Cook" or "Rice" option of the rice cooker. *(3)* Hot chicken mafaldine, topped with grated Parmesan, is ready to be served.

213.   CHICKEN ANELLINI

Total Time: 30 minutes | Prep Time: 10 minutes

Ingredients:

1 cup anellini pasta

2 boneless, skinless

chicken breasts, diced
1 tablespoon olive oil

1 small onion, finely

2 cloves garlic, minced

1 teaspoon dried oregano

Grated Parmesan cheese for garnish

chopped

1 can (14 ounces) diced tomatoes

Salt and pepper to taste

Directions:

(1) Cook anellini pasta in the rice cooker according to the package directions. *(2)* Meanwhile, heat olive oil in a middle pan.

Diced chicken should be browned and cooked thoroughly in 5-6 minutes . Remove chicken from pan and put aside. *(3)* Add chopped onion & minced garlic to the skillet. Sauté for 2-3 minutes to soften. *(4)* Add dried oregano, salt, pepper, and chopped tomatoes with juices to the skillet. Mix well. *(5)* Return cooked chicken to pan & simmer for 5 minutes. *(6)* Add cooked pasta to the pan with chicken and sauce, draining any excess water. Mix thoroughly. *(7)* Sprinkle Parmesan cheese over the top & serve warm.

214.   CREAM OF MUSHROOM SOUP

Total Time: 30 minutes | Prep Time: 10 minutes

Ingredients:

1 tablespoon butter

8 ounces mushrooms, sliced

1 cup heavy cream

Chopped fresh parsley for garnish (optional)

1 small onion, finely chopped

2 cups chicken or vegetable broth

Salt and pepper to taste

Directions:

(1) Butter should be melted in the rice cooker.
(2) Toss in some sliced mushrooms and

minced onion. After around 5 or 6 minutes of sautéing, the mushrooms should be soft, and the onion should be transparent. *(3)* Simmer after adding broth (chicken or veggie). *(4)* While continually swirling, slowly pour in the heavy cream. *(5)* Taste & add salt & pepper as needed. *(6)* Stirring periodically, continue simmering the soup for another 7 to 10 minutes or until it reaches a little thick consistency. *(7)* If preferred, serve hot with chopped fresh parsley as a garnish.

215.   CHICKEN GNOCCHI

Total Time: 30 minutes | Prep Time: 10 minutes

Ingredients:

1 pound potato gnocchi

1 tablespoon olive oil

2 cloves garlic, minced

Salt and pepper to taste

2 boneless, skinless chicken breasts, diced

1 cup spinach leaves

1 cup marinara sauce

Grated Parmesan cheese for garnish

Directions:

(1) Cook potato gnocchi in the rice cooker according to package directions. *(2)*

Meanwhile, warm olive oil in a medium pan. Diced chicken should be browned and cooked thoroughly in 5-6 minutes . Remove chicken from pan and put aside. *(3)* In the same skillet, sauté minced garlic for 1 minute until fragrant. *(4)* Put spinach in the pan and heat for 2-3 minutes until wilted. *(5)* Put cooked chicken back in the pan and add marinara. Mix well and boil for 2-3 minutes. *(6)* Add cooked gnocchi to the pan with chicken and sauce, draining any excess water. Mix thoroughly. *(7)* Sprinkle Parmesan cheese over the top & serve warm.

216.   BABA GHANOUSH

Ingredients:

2 large eggplants	2 cloves garlic, minced
2 tablespoons tahini	2 tablespoons lemon juice
2 tablespoons olive oil	Salt and pepper to taste
Chopped fresh parsley for garnish (optional)	Pita bread or crackers for serving

Directions:

(1) Before adding the eggplants to the rice cooker, pierce them with a fork. After 20 to 25 minutes of steaming, the eggplants should be soft. *(2)* Take the cooked eggplants out of the rice cooker and let them cool for a little while. *(3)* Take the eggplants and remove their skins. Then, put the meat in a basin. To get a smooth puree, use a fork to mash the eggplant. *(4)* Season the mashed eggplant with salt, pepper, lemon juice, tahini, olive oil, and chopped garlic. Mix thoroughly. *(5)* Serve with pita bread or crackers & if preferred, garnish with chopped fresh parsley. Transfer the baba ghanoush to a serving dish.

217. CHICKEN PENNE

Total Time: 30 minutes | Prep Time: 10 minutes

Ingredients:

2 cups penne pasta	1 cup diced chicken breast
1 cup diced bell peppers	1 cup diced onions
1 can (14 oz) diced tomatoes	2 cloves garlic, minced
2 cups chicken broth	1 teaspoon dried oregano
Salt and pepper to taste	

Directions:

(1) In a rice cooker, combine penne pasta, chicken breast, diced bell peppers, onions, tomatoes, garlic, chicken broth, dried oregano, salt, and pepper. *(2)* Make sure to mix everything well. *(3)* Turn the rice cooker to the "Quick Cook" or "White Rice" option, then cover and close the lid. *(4)* After 20 minutes of cooking, the pasta should be soft, and the chicken should be cooked all the way through. *(5)* Carefully remove the cover and give the chicken penne a quick swirl before serving.

218. CHICKEN POT PIE

Total Time: 30 minutes | Prep Time: 10 minutes

Ingredients:

1 cup cooked chicken, shredded	1 cup mixed frozen vegetables
1 cup chicken broth	1 can cream of chicken soup
1 teaspoon dried thyme	Salt and pepper to taste
1 sheet of pre-made puff pastry, thawed	

Directions:

(1) Stir together the cooked chicken, a variety of frozen veggies, chicken broth, chicken soup, dried thyme, pepper, salt, and rice in the rice cooker. *(2)* Stir until fully combined. *(3)* After adding the chicken mixture to the rice cooker pot, lay the pre-made puff pastry layer on top, removing any extra if necessary. *(4)* Turn the rice cooker to the "Quick Cook" or "White Rice" option, then cover and close the lid. *(5)* Puff pastry should be golden brown, and the

filling should be bubbling after 20 minutes in the oven. *(6)* Take the pot out of the rice cooker with care and let it aside to cool for a while before serving.

219. MACARONI AND CHEESE

Total Time: 30 minutes | Prep Time: 5 minutes

Ingredients:

2 cups elbow macaroni

2 cups milk

1 teaspoon mustard powder

2 cups shredded cheddar cheese

2 tablespoons butter

Salt and pepper to taste

Directions:

(1) While the rice is cooking, throw in the elbow macaroni, shredded cheddar, milk, butter, mustard powder, salt, and pepper. *(2)* Make sure to mix everything well. *(3)* Turn the rice cooker to the "Quick Cook" or "White Rice" option, then cover and close the lid. *(4)* Be sure to toss the macaroni every so often while it cooks for 20 minutes to melt the cheese. *(5)* Macaroni and cheese should be served hot once cooked.

220. BEEF BOURGUIGNON

Total Time: 30 minutes | Prep Time: 10 minutes

Ingredients:

1 pound beef stew meat, cubed

1 cup diced onions

1 cup beef broth

2 tablespoons tomato paste

1 teaspoon dried thyme

1 cup sliced mushrooms

2 cloves garlic, minced

1 cup red wine

1 tablespoon Worcestershire sauce

Salt and pepper to taste

Directions:

(1) Add the following ingredients to the rice cooker pot: beef stew meat, chopped onions, minced garlic, beef broth, tomato paste, Worcestershire sauce, dried thyme, salt, and pepper. *(2)* Make sure to mix everything well. *(3)* Turn the rice cooker to the "Quick Cook" or "White Rice" option, then cover and close the lid. *(4)* Stirring periodically, simmer the meat for 20 minutes or until it is soft and fully cooked. *(5)* Stir in the prepared rice or mashed potatoes and top with the meat bourguignon. Serve immediately.

221. SAAG PANEER

Total Time: 30 minutes | Prep Time: 10 minutes

Ingredients:

1 cup spinach, chopped

1 onion, finely chopped

2 cloves garlic, minced

1 teaspoon cumin seeds

200g paneer, cubed

2 tomatoes, pureed

1 teaspoon ginger, grated

1 teaspoon garam masala

1/2 teaspoon turmeric powder

2 tablespoons oil

Salt to taste

Directions:

(1) Turn the rice cooker to sauté mode and heat up the oil. *(2)* Bring the cumin seeds to a crackling boil. *(3)* Chopped garlic, ginger, and onions should be added. Brown the onions in a skillet over middle heat. *(4)* Garnish with salt,

turmeric powder, and tomato puree. Thicken the mixture by cooking it. *(5)* Add the paneer cubes and chopped spinach and mix well. After

10 minutes of cooking, cover and let cook. *(6)* Toss in some garam masala and top with hot rice or naan.

222.   MAPLE GLAZED SALMON

Total Time: 25 minutes | Prep Time: 5 minutes

Ingredients:

2 salmon fillets	2 tablespoons maple syrup
1 tablespoon soy sauce	1 tablespoon lemon juice
Salt and pepper to taste	

Directions:

(1) Blend together the soy sauce, maple syrup, lemon juice, salt & pepper in a mixing bowl. *(2)* Coat the salmon fillets with the mixture. *(3)* Before you put the cover on the rice cooker, add the fillets. *(4)* Sauté the salmon for around fifteen to twenty minutes or until it reaches the desired doneness. *(5)* Top with rice or steamed veggies and serve hot.

223.   CHICKEN BIGOLI

Total Time: 30 minutes | Prep Time: 10 minutes

Ingredients:

250g bigoli pasta	2 chicken breasts, diced
1 onion, chopped	2 cloves garlic, minced
1 bell pepper, sliced	1 cup tomato sauce
1 teaspoon dried oregano	Salt and pepper to taste
2 tablespoons olive oil	

Directions:

(1) Before setting aside, cook the bigoli pasta according to the package directions. *(2)* While the rice cooker is on the sauté setting, heat the olive oil. *(3)* Toss in the minced garlic & onions & cook until softened. *(4)* Before they brown, add the diced chicken breasts. *(5)* Next, add the tomato sauce, chopped bell pepper, dry oregano, salt, and pepper. Mix well. *(6)* Ten minutes of steam cooking with the lid closed should do the trick. *(7)* Toss with cooked bigoli pasta and serve hot.

224.   LEMON PEPPER CHICKEN

Total Time: 30 minutes | Prep Time: 10 minutes

Ingredients:

4 chicken thighs	2 tablespoons lemon juice
1 teaspoon lemon zest	1 teaspoon black pepper
1 teaspoon garlic powder	Salt to taste
2 tablespoons olive oil	

Directions:

(1) In a bowl, mix the olive oil, pepper, salt, garlic powder, zest & juice from two lemons. *(2)* Coat the chicken thighs equally by rubbing the mixture on them. *(3)* Seal the rice cooker and add the chicken thighs. *(4)* The chicken should be cooked thoroughly after 20 minutes of steaming. *(5)* Warm and serve with roasted veggies or a side salad.

225. TIROPITA

Total Time: 30 minutes | Prep Time: 10 minutes

Ingredients:

1 cup crumbled feta cheese

1 cup shredded mozzarella cheese

1/4 cup chopped fresh parsley

1/4 cup chopped green onions

1/4 teaspoon black pepper

6 sheets phyllo dough, thawed if frozen

1/4 cup melted butter

Directions:

(1) Start your rice cooker on "Cook" mode. *(2)* Mix feta, mozzarella, parsley, green onions, and black pepper in a bowl. *(3)* Melt the butter and brush it over one sheet of phyllo dough set on a clean board. Put another phyllo dough layer on top and butter it. Repeat until three papers are stacked. *(4)* Cut the layered phyllo dough into six equal squares. *(5)* Center each square with a tablespoon of cheese mixture. *(6)* Create little packages by folding square corners toward the center. *(7)* Place tiro pitas in a rice cooker basket in a single layer. *(8)* Close the rice cooker lid and cook tiro pitas for 10-15 minutes until golden brown and crispy. *(9)* Serve hot and enjoy!

226. ROAST BEEF SANDWICH

Total Time: 25 minutes | Prep Time: 10 minutes

Ingredients:

½ pound thinly sliced roast beef

4 slices provolone cheese

4 sandwich rolls

¼ cup mayonnaise

2 tablespoons prepared horseradish

Salt and pepper to taste

Lettuce leaves

Sliced tomatoes

Sliced red onions

Directions:

*(1)*Set the "Cook" setting on your rice cooker to preheat it. *(2)* The mayonnaise and horseradish should be combined in a small bowl. Taste & add salt & pepper as needed. *(3)* Distribute the mayonnaise mixture evenly over the bottom halves of the halved sandwich buns. *(4)* Start by spreading the roast meat and provolone cheese evenly over the bottom half of each bun. *(5)* Serve topped with sliced onion, tomato, and lettuce. *(6)* Arrange the sandwich tops on top of the roll halves. *(7)* Wrap each sandwich in aluminum foil separately. *(8)* After you've wrapped each sandwich, put them in the rice cooker. *(9)* To heat the sandwiches and melt the cheese, cover and cook for 10 to fifteen minutes . *(10)* Slice open the sandwiches, top with spicy sauce, and enjoy!

227. CHICKEN WRAPS

Total Time: 30 minutes | Prep Time: 15 minutes

Ingredients:

2 boneless, skinless chicken breasts

½ cup Greek yogurt

2 tablespoons lemon juice

1 teaspoon garlic powder

Salt and pepper to taste

4 large flour tortillas

1 cup shredded lettuce

1 cup diced tomatoes

½ cup crumbled feta cheese

Tzatziki sauce (optional)

(1) Shred the chicken and mix it with the Greek yogurt, lemon juice, garlic powder, salt, and pepper in a mixing bowl. (2) Just a few minutes on "Cook" in the rice cooker will warm the flour tortillas. (3) Top each tortilla with some of the chicken mixture. (4) Pile on the feta crumbles, chopped tomatoes, and shredded lettuce. (5) Garnish with tzatziki sauce if you want. (6) Wrap the filling in the tortillas by rolling them up and folding the edges in. (7) Enjoy right away after serving!

228.   GREEK SALAD

Total Time: 20 minutes | Prep Time: 10 minutes

Ingredients:

2 large tomatoes, diced

1 cucumber, diced

½ red onion, thinly sliced

½ cup Kalamata olives

½ cup crumbled feta cheese

2 tablespoons extra virgin olive oil

1 tablespoon red wine vinegar

1 teaspoon dried oregano

Salt and pepper to taste

Directions:

(1) Throw in some chopped cucumber, red onion, Kalamata olives, crumbled feta cheese, and diced tomatoes in a big bowl. (2) Melt the red wine vinegar, olive oil, dried oregano, salt, & pepper in a small bowl. Whisk in the vinegar. (3) After adding the dressing, toss the salad to coat it evenly. (4) As soon as it's prepared, serve it as a light lunch or side dish. Have fun!

229.   CHICKEN KEBABS

Total Time: 30 minutes | Prep Time: 15 minutes

Ingredients:

1 lb chicken breast, cut into cubes

1 red bell pepper, cut into chunks

1 green bell pepper, cut into chunks

1 onion, cut into chunks

2 tablespoons olive oil

2 tablespoons lemon juice

1 teaspoon paprika

Salt and pepper to taste

Directions:

(1) Set the rice cooker to sauté before you begin. (2) Toss the olive oil, paprika, lemon juice, salt, and pepper in a bowl. (3) Skewer the chicken, diced bell peppers, and chopped onion. (4) Combine the olive oil and brush it onto the skewers. (5) Toss the skewers into the rice cooker and simmer, stirring periodically, for 10 to 12 minutes or until the chicken is cooked through. (6) Top with your preferred dipping sauce and serve hot.

230.   HERB CRUSTED SALMON

Total Time: 25 minutes | Prep Time: 10 minutes

Ingredients:

4 salmon fillets

2 tablespoons olive oil

2 cloves garlic, minced

1 tablespoon chopped fresh parsley

1 tablespoon

Salt and pepper to

chopped fresh dill   taste

Directions:

(1) Add salt & pepper to the salmon fillets. (2) Combine the garlic, parsley, dill, and olive oil in a small bowl. (3) Distribute the herb mixture

evenly over the salmon fillets. *(4)* Before serving, cook the salmon fillets in a rice cooker for 12–15 minutes or until opaque throughout. *(5)* Heat and garnish with lemon wedges.

231.   SHRIMP COCKTAIL

Total Time: 20 minutes | Prep Time: 10 minutes

Ingredients:

1 lb large shrimp, peeled and deveined	1 lemon, halved
1/4 cup ketchup	2 tablespoons prepared horseradish
1 tablespoon Worcestershire sauce	Salt and pepper to taste

Directions:

(1) Add half a lemon juice to the water in the rice cooker. *(2)* After getting a steamed basket ready, drop the shrimp in and set the rice cooker to cook. *(3)* Sauté the shrimp for about five to seven minutes , or until they become pink and are opaque throughout. *(4)* To create the cocktail sauce, combine the ketchup, horseradish, Worcestershire sauce, salt & pepper in a small bowl. *(5)* Arrange the shrimp on a platter and top with cocktail sauce and lemon wedges.

232.   SALMON TERIYAKI

Total Time: 30 minutes | Prep Time: 10 minutes

Ingredients:

4 salmon fillets	1/4 cup soy sauce
2 tablespoons honey	2 cloves garlic, minced
1 teaspoon grated ginger	1 tablespoon sesame seeds (optional)

Directions:

(1) The teriyaki sauce is made by combining soy sauce, honey, garlic & ginger in a small bowl. *(2)* After seasoning the salmon fillets, add them to the rice cooker along with the teriyaki sauce. *(3)* To cook the salmon, cover the rice cooker and cook on steam for 15 to 18 minutes or until it reaches the desired doneness. *(4)* Before serving, top with sesame seeds if you want.

233.   TOMATO BASIL SOUP

Total Time: 30 minutes | Prep Time: 10 minutes

Ingredients:

2 cups canned diced tomatoes	1 cup vegetable broth
1/4 cup chopped fresh basil	2 cloves garlic, minced
1 tablespoon olive oil	Salt and pepper to taste
1/4 cup heavy cream (optional)	Grated Parmesan cheese for garnish (optional)

Directions:

(1) While the rice cooker is set to sauté, heat the olive oil. *(2)* After a minute of sautéing, add the minced garlic. *(3)* Blend in the veggie broth and chopped tomatoes. Mix thoroughly. *(4)* Place the cover on top of the rice cooker and cook on high heat for 15 minutes . *(5)* After the simmering time is over, add the heavy cream and chopped basil. *(6)* Taste & add salt & pepper as needed. *(7)* If preferred,

serve hot with grated Parmesan cheese as a garnish.

234. CHICKEN MANICOTTI

Total Time: 30 minutes | Prep Time: 15 minutes

Ingredients:

8 manicotti shells	1 cup cooked chicken, shredded
1 cup ricotta cheese	1/2 cup shredded mozzarella cheese
1/4 cup grated Parmesan cheese	1 egg, beaten
1 teaspoon Italian seasoning	1 cup marinara sauce
Salt and pepper to taste	Fresh parsley for garnish (optional)

Directions:

(1) Drain and put aside the cooked manicotti shells; then, proceed as directed on the box. (2) The shredded chicken, ricotta, mozzarella, Parmesan, beaten egg, Italian seasoning, salt, and pepper should all be combined in a bowl. (3) After the manicotti are cooked, stuff them with the chicken and cheese mixture. (4) Coat the base of the rice cooker with marinara sauce. (5) Spread the sauce evenly over the manicotti shells and arrange them in a single layer. (6) Place the cover on top of the rice cooker and cook on high heat for 15 minutes . (7) Carefully use tongs to remove the manicotti after it's done. (8) If desired, top right before serving with a sprinkling of fresh parsley.

235. CHICKEN SALAD

Total Time: 20 minutes | Prep Time: 10 minutes

Ingredients:

2 cups cooked chicken breast, shredded	1/2 cup mayonnaise
1/4 cup Greek yogurt	1 stalk celery, finely chopped
1/4 cup red onion, finely chopped	1/4 cup grapes, halved
1/4 cup almonds, chopped	Salt and pepper to taste
Lettuce leaves for serving (optional)	Sliced bread or rolls for serving (optional)

Directions:

(1) Combine the cut celery, red onion, grapes, and almonds with the shredded chicken, mayonnaise, Greek yogurt, and chopped nuts in a big bowl. (2) Taste & add salt & pepper as needed. (3) Layer lettuce leaves on top of the chicken salad, or use it as a sandwich filling between two slices of bread or rolls.

236. CAPRESE SANDWICH

Total Time: 15 minutes | Prep Time: 5 minutes

Ingredients:

4 slices of bread	2 tomatoes, thinly sliced
4 slices fresh mozzarella cheese	1/4 cup fresh basil leaves
2 tablespoons balsamic glaze	Salt and pepper to taste

Directions:

(1) Spread some fresh mozzarella cheese over the bread. (2) Finish with a sprinkle of fresh basil leaves and thinly sliced tomatoes. (3) Finish with a balsamic glaze. (4) Taste & add salt & pepper as needed. (5) Press the sandwich tops down and set the rice cooker to

cook. *(6)* Put the cover on the rice cooker & cook it for 5 minutes . *(7)* Carefully take the sandwiches out of the oven and serve hot.

237. CHICKEN BUSIATE

Total Time: 30 minutes | Prep Time: 10 minutes

Ingredients:

1 lb chicken breast, diced

1 onion, chopped

1 can (14 oz) diced tomatoes

1 teaspoon dried oregano

2 cups busiate pasta

2 cloves garlic, minced

1 cup chicken broth

Salt and pepper to taste

Directions:

(1) In a rice cooker, combine the following Ingredients: chicken, busiate pasta, onion, garlic, tomatoes (with juice), chicken broth, dried oregano, salt, and pepper. *(2)* Mix thoroughly. *(3)* After placing the cover on top, turn the rice cooker to the rapid cook option. *(4)* Carefully remove the cover and mix the chicken broth after the cooking cycle is finished. *(5)* Warm up and savor!

238. CHICKEN RAVIOLI

Total Time: 25 minutes | Prep Time: 5 minutes

Ingredients:

1 lb chicken thighs, boneless and skinless

1 jar (16 oz) marinara sauce

Salt and pepper to taste

2 cups cheese ravioli

1 teaspoon Italian seasoning

Directions:

(1) Make little pieces of the chicken thighs. *(2)* In a rice cooker, combine the ravioli filled with cheese, chicken thighs, marinara sauce, Italian seasoning, salt, and pepper. *(3)* Mix thoroughly. *(4)* After placing the cover on top, turn the rice cooker to the rapid cook option. *(5)* Gently remove the cover and mix the chicken ravioli after the cooking time is over. *(6)* If you'd like, top it with grated Parmesan cheese and serve it hot.

239. CHICKEN CACCIATORE

Total Time: 30 minutes | Prep Time: 10 minutes

Ingredients:

1 lb chicken drumsticks

1 bell pepper, sliced

1 can (14 oz) crushed tomatoes

1 teaspoon dried oregano

1 onion, sliced

2 cloves garlic, minced

1 teaspoon dried basil

Salt and pepper to taste

Directions:

(1) Put the following ingredients into the rice cooker: chicken drumsticks, onion, bell pepper, garlic, smashed tomatoes, dried basil, dried oregano, salt, and pepper. *(2)* Mix thoroughly. *(3)* After placing the cover on top, turn the rice cooker to the rapid cook option. *(4)* Stir the chicken cacciatore when the cooking cycle is finished by gently opening the

cover. *(5)* Top with cooked spaghetti or serve hot with crusty toast.

240.   CHICKEN SCARPARIELLO

Total Time: 25 minutes | Prep Time: 5 minutes

Ingredients:

1 lb chicken breast, sliced	1 cup baby potatoes, halved
1 cup cherry tomatoes	1/2 cup chicken broth
2 tablespoons olive oil	2 cloves garlic, minced
1 teaspoon crushed red pepper flakes	Salt and pepper to taste

Directions:

(1) In a skillet set over middle heat, warm the olive oil. Before adding the cut chicken breast, brown it on both sides. *(2)* Place the chicken breasts in the rice cooker when they have cooked. *(3)* Toss in some chopped garlic, cherry tomatoes, salt, pepper, and baby potatoes in the same pan. Brown for three to four minutes . *(4)* Add the sautéed veggies and chicken to the rice cooker. *(5)* Add chicken broth to the saucepan. *(6)* After placing the cover on top, turn the rice cooker to the rapid cook option. *(7)* Remove the lid and stir the chicken scarpariello gently when the timer goes off. *(8)* Warm it up and top it off with some chopped fresh parsley.

241.   TUNA SALAD

Total Time: 15 minutes | Prep Time: 10 minutes

Ingredients:

2 cans of tuna, drained	1/4 cup mayonnaise
2 tablespoons lemon juice	1/4 cup diced celery
1/4 cup diced red onion	Salt and pepper to taste
Optional: chopped parsley for garnish	

Directions:

(1) Throw the drained tuna, mayonnaise, lemon juice, celery, and red onion into a bowl and stir to incorporate. Thoroughly combine. *(2)* Taste & add salt & pepper as needed. *(3)* Put it in a sandwich or scatter it over some lettuce and serve right away. *(4)* If you'd like, you may top it off with chopped parsley.

242.   SKORDALIA

Total Time: 20 minutes | Prep Time: 10 minutes

Ingredients:

2 large potatoes, peeled and chopped	4 cloves garlic, minced
1/4 cup olive oil	2 tablespoons lemon juice
Salt to taste	Optnl: chopped fresh parsley for garnish

Directions:

(1) In the rice cooker pot, add the chopped potatoes and cover with water. The potatoes should be cooked for about 10 minutes on the "Steam" option or until they are soft. *(2)* After draining, place the potatoes in a mixing dish. Get them as smooth as possible by mashing them with a fork or a potato masher. *(3)* Incorporate the lemon juice, olive oil, and chopped garlic into the mashed potatoes. Stir until fully combined. *(4)* As a seasoning, add salt to taste. *(5)* If preferred, top the Skordalia with chopped fresh parsley and serve as a dip or spread.

243. BBQ PULLED PORK

Total Time: 30 minutes | Prep Time: 5 minutes

Ingredients:

1 pound pork shoulder, trimmed and cut into chunks

1/2 cup chicken broth

Hamburger buns or sandwich rolls for serving

1 cup BBQ sauce

Salt and pepper to taste

Directions:

(1) Add salt and pepper to the pork pieces. *(2)* Along with the chicken stock and BBQ sauce, add the seasoned pork pieces to the rice cooker pot. *(3)* After placing the cover back on the rice cooker, choose either the "Quick Cook" or "Pressure Cook" option. Simmer for half an hour. *(4)* After the rice cooker's cooking cycle is over, carefully follow the directions to release the pressure. *(5)* Shred the cooked pork with two forks as the rice cooks. *(6)* Sandwich or hamburger buns are perfect for serving the BBQ pulled pork.

244. CHICKEN PENNE VODKA

Total Time: 30 minutes | Prep Time: 10 minutes

Ingredients:

8 oz penne pasta

2 boneless, skinless chicken breasts, diced

1/4 cup vodka

1/2 cup heavy cream

Grated Parmesan cheese for serving

1 tablespoon olive oil

2 cloves garlic, minced

1 cup tomato sauce

Salt and pepper to taste

Directions:

(1) Make sure the penne pasta is cooked al dente per the package directions. Rinse and reserve. *(2)* In the rice cooker, heat the olive oil by using the "Sauté" setting. *(3)* Put the minced garlic and diced chicken breasts in the saucepan. Cook the poultry until the interior is no longer raw in a skillet. *(4)* Simmer the vodka for one to two minutes to facilitate the evaporation of the alcohol. *(5)* Heavier cream and tomato sauce should be added to the saucepan. Mix thoroughly. *(6)* Add salt & pepper to the sauce according to your taste. *(7)* After the penne is done, add it to the sauce in the rice cooker and toss to coat. *(8)* Hot Chicken Penne Vodka should be garnished with a layer of grated Parmesan cheese.

245. CHICKEN PARMIGIANA

Total Time: 30 minutes | Prep Time: 10 minutes

Ingredients:

2 boneless, skinless chicken breasts

1/2 cup grated Parmesan cheese

1 cup shredded mozzarella cheese

1 cup breadcrumbs

1 cup marinara sauce

Salt and pepper to taste

Directions:

(1) Pepper and salt the chicken breasts. *(2)* Combine the breadcrumbs and Parmesan on a shallow plate. *(3)* Add breadcrumb mixture to each chicken breast and coat. *(4)* Bring the rice cooker to a boil on the sauté setting. Include

one tablespoon of oil. *(5)* Brown the chicken breasts in a rice cooker for five to seven minutes on each side. *(6)* Coat the chicken with marinara sauce. *(7)* Shred some mozzarella cheese and sprinkle it on top. *(8)* Ten minutes of cooking time should be enough to melt the cheese & cook the chicken well in a rice cooker. Be sure to cover the lid. *(9)* Top with your preferred side and serve hot.

246.   BEEF KEBABS

Total Time: 25 minutes | Prep Time: 15 minutes

Ingredients:

1 lb beef sirloin, cut into cubes

1 onion, cut into chunks

2 tablespoons olive oil

Salt and pepper to taste

1 bell pepper, cut into chunks

1/4 cup soy sauce

2 cloves garlic, minced

Directions:

(1) Combine the soy sauce, olive oil, garlic powder, salt, and pepper in a mixing bowl. *(2)* After 10 minutes , stir in the meat cubes to the marinade. *(3)* Skewer the onion, bell pepper, and meat cubes. *(4)* Bring the rice cooker to a boil on the sauté setting. Include one tablespoon of oil. *(5)* After adding the kebabs to the rice cooker, simmer for 5 to 7 minutes, stirring once or twice, or until the meat reaches the doneness you choose. *(6)* Accompanied with hot rice or salad.

247.   CHICKEN TAGLIATELLE

Total Time: 30 minutes | Prep Time: 10 minutes

Ingredients:

8 oz tagliatelle pasta

1 cup sliced mushrooms

1/2 cup grated Parmesan cheese

Salt and pepper to taste

2 boneless, skinless chicken breasts, diced

1 cup heavy cream

2 tablespoons butter

Directions:

(1) Prepare the tagliatelle pasta as directed on the box. Rinse and reserve. *(2)* Bring the rice cooker to a boil on the sauté setting. Put the butter in. *(3)* In a rice cooker, brown the diced chicken breasts for five to seven minutes . *(4)* Saute the sliced mushrooms for a further three to four minutes. *(5)* Drizzle with the heavy cream and sprinkle with the grated Parmesan. Mix thoroughly. *(6)* After the tagliatelle is done, add it to the rice cooker and mix until evenly coated. *(7)* Taste & add salt & pepper as needed. *(8)* If you'd like, top it with more Parmesan cheese and serve it hot.

248.   CHICKEN FRIED RICE

Total Time: 20 minutes | Prep Time: 10 minutes

Ingredients:

2 cups cooked rice

2 boneless, skinless chicken thighs, diced

1 cup mixed vegetables (peas, carrots, corn)

2 tablespoons soy

2 eggs, beaten

2 tablespoons sesame

sauce

2 cloves garlic, minced

oil

Salt and pepper to taste

Directions:

(1) Bring the rice cooker to a boil on the sauté setting. Include one tablespoon of oil. **(2)** In the rice cooker, combine chopped chicken thighs with minced garlic. Keep cooking for another 5 to 7 minutes or until the chicken is done. **(3)** Place the beaten eggs in the rice cooker and push the chicken to one side. Cook the eggs in a skillet until they're done. **(4)** After the rice has cooked for two or three minutes, add the mixed veggies. **(5)** Combine cooked rice, soy sauce, and sesame oil; stir to combine. Thoroughly combine. **(6)** Taste & add salt & pepper as needed. **(7)** To ensure thorough heating, cook for another two or three minutes. **(8)** Whether you like it hot or cold, top with chopped green onions and serve.

249. HAM AND CHEESE SANDWICH

Total Time: 15 minutes | Prep Time: 5 minutes

Ingredients:

4 slices of bread

4 slices of cheese (cheddar or your choice)

4 slices of ham

Butter or margarine

Directions:

(1) On a level surface, lay down two pieces of bread. **(2)** Spread ham and cheese on top of each. **(3)** Serve topped with the remaining pieces of bread. **(4)** In a nonstick skillet, melt a small amount of butter over medium heat. **(5)** Toast the bread and cheese in a pan over medium heat for two or three minutes on each side or until the sandwiches are cooked through. **(6)** Warm up and savor!

250. CHICKEN SEDANI

Total Time: 25 minutes | Prep Time: 10 minutes

Ingredients:

2 boneless, skinless chicken breasts

1 cup diced tomatoes

2 cloves garlic, minced

Salt and pepper to taste

2 cups sedan pasta

1 cup chicken broth

1 teaspoon dried oregano

Grated Parmesan cheese (optional)

Directions:

(1) Add the chopped tomatoes, chicken broth, dried oregano, minced garlic, and sedani pasta to the rice cooker. **(2)** Before topping the spaghetti with the chicken pieces, season them with salt and pepper. **(3)** Turn the rice cooker to the "Quick Cook" or "White Rice" option, then cover and close the lid. **(4)** Once the timer expires, remove the cover and proceed to agitate the contents. **(5)** Warm before serving, with grated Parmesan cheese on top if desired.

251. BAKED SALMON

Total Time: 20 minutes | Prep Time: 5 minutes

Ingredients:

2 salmon fillets

2 tablespoons soy sauce

1 tablespoon honey

1 teaspoon minced
garlic

Lemon wedges for
serving

1 teaspoon minced
ginger

Salt and pepper to
taste

After seasoning the salmon fillets, add them to the rice cooker and coat them evenly with the sauce. *(3)* Add a little salt & pepper to taste. *(4)* After placing the rice cooker on the "Steam" or "Quick Cook" mode, cover it and close the lid. *(5)* Take the salmon out of the rice cooker after it's done cooking, and top it with lemon wedges.

Directions:

(1) Combine the soy sauce, honey, minced garlic, & ginger in a small bowl & mix well. *(2)*

252.   MINESTRONE SOUP

Total Time: 30 minutes | Prep Time: 10 minutes

Ingredients:

4 cups chicken or vegetable broth	1 can (14 oz) diced tomatoes
1 cup diced carrots	1 cup diced celery
1 cup diced zucchini	1 cup cooked small pasta
1 can (14 oz) kidney beans, drained and rinsed	2 cloves garlic, minced
1 teaspoon dried thyme	Salt and pepper to taste
Grated Parmesan cheese for serving (optional)	

Directions:

(1) Throw everything into the rice cooker: broth (chicken or veggie), chopped tomatoes, carrots, celery, zucchini, kidney beans, cooked pasta, minced garlic, and dried thyme. *(2)* After placing the rice cooker on the "Soup" or "Quick Cook" option, make sure to close the lid. *(3)* When the veggies are soft and the soup is hot, add salt & pepper to taste. *(4)* Warm before serving, with grated Parmesan cheese on top if desired.

253.   BRIAM

Total Time: 30 minutes | Prep Time: 10 minutes

Ingredients:

2 medium-sized potatoes, peeled and diced	1 eggplant, diced
1 zucchini, diced	1 red bell pepper, diced
1 yellow bell pepper, diced	1 onion, diced
2 cloves garlic, minced	2 tomatoes, diced
2 tablespoons olive oil	Salt and pepper to taste

Directions:

(1) In the rice cooker, add all of the chopped veggies. *(2)* After seasoning the veggies with salt and pepper, drizzle them with olive oil. *(3)* After placing the cover on top of the rice cooker, turn it to the "cook" setting. *(4)* After adding the veggies, toss them regularly and let them simmer for 20 minutes or until they are cooked. *(5)* Hot Briam may be a main meal or a side dish after it's prepared.

254.   POTATO SKINS

Total Time: 30 minutes | Prep Time: 10 minutes

Ingredients:

4 large russet   1 cup shredded

potatoes
4 slices bacon, cooked and crumbled
2 green onions, chopped

cheddar cheese
1/4 cup sour cream

Salt and pepper to taste

Directions:

(1) Put all of the chopped vegetables into the rice cooker. *(2)* Drizzle olive oil over the vegetables after seasoning them with pepper and salt. *(3)* Cover the rice cooker & activate the "cook" function. *(4)* Simmer the vegetables for 20 minutes or until tender, stirring occasionally after adding them. *(5)* As it is, hot bream may be either a main course or a side dish.

255. LAMB KEBABS

Total Time: 30 minutes | Prep Time: 15 minutes

Ingredients:

1 lb lamb meat, cubed
2 tablespoons olive oil

1 teaspoon ground cumin
Salt and pepper to taste

1 onion, chopped
2 cloves garlic, minced

1 teaspoon paprika

Directions:

(1) The lamb cubes, chopped onion, minced garlic, olive oil, cumin, paprika, salt, and pepper should all be mixed together in a bowl. *(2)* Thread skewers with the seasoned cubes of lamb. *(3)* After threading the skewers, put the rice cooker to the "grill" option and cook, stirring regularly, for 10 to 15 minutes or until the lamb is tender. *(4)* The lamb kebabs, after grilled, are best served hot with a side dish of your choosing.

256. CHICKEN LASAGNETTE

Total Time: 30 minutes | Prep Time: 10 minutes

Ingredients:

1 lb boneless, skinless chicken breasts, diced
2 cloves garlic, minced
8 oz lasagna noodles broken into pieces
1/4 cup grated Parmesan cheese

1 onion, chopped

2 cups marinara sauce

1 cup shredded mozzarella cheese
Salt and pepper to taste

Directions:

(1) Saute the minced garlic & chopped onion in the rice cooker until they are tender. *(2)* Before cooking the rice, brown the chopped chicken breast. *(3)* Make sure the lasagna noodles are well covered in sauce by stirring in the marinara sauce and broken noodles. *(4)* Cook the noodles on the "simmer" setting for 15 to 20 minutes , stirring frequently, with the lid on, or until tender. *(5)* Shredded mozzarella and grated Parmesan should be sprinkled on top of cooked noodles. *(6)* To make sure the cheese melts and bubbles, cover and simmer for another 5 minutes. *(7)* Top with chopped fresh parsley & serve hot.

257. CHICKEN CAESAR WRAP

Total Time: 25 minutes | Prep Time: 10 minutes

Ingredients:

1 boneless, skinless chicken breast	Salt and pepper to taste
2 tablespoons Caesar dressing	1 cup shredded romaine lettuce
1/4 cup grated Parmesan cheese	2 large flour tortillas

Directions:

(1) Add salt & pepper to the chicken breast. **(2)** Season the chicken breast with Caesar dressing and add it to the rice cooker. **(3)** After 20 minutes of cooking, cover the rice cooker and remove the lid. **(4)** By employing two utensils, shred the cooked poultry. Put the tortillas in the rice cooker and heat them for a minute or two. **(5)** Layer the romaine lettuce, Parmesan cheese, shredded chicken, and tortillas to make the wraps. **(6)** Tightly roll the wraps and serve right away.

258. CHICKEN PICI

Total Time: 30 minutes | Prep Time: 10 minutes

Ingredients:

1 boneless, skinless chicken breast	Salt and pepper to taste
1 cup pici pasta	1 cup cherry tomatoes, halved
2 cloves garlic, minced	1/4 cup chopped fresh basil
2 tablespoons olive oil	

Directions:

(1) Add salt & pepper to the chicken breast. **(2)** Throw the chicken breast, pici pasta, cherry tomatoes, garlic powder, basil leaves, and olive oil into the rice cooker. Next, add the minced garlic. **(3)** Pour in just enough water to submerge the items. **(4)** Put the rice cooker cover on and simmer for 25 minutes . **(5)** Take the chicken breast out of the oven and shred it with two forks when the cooking cycle has finished. **(6)** Reintegrate the chicken shreds into the spaghetti sauce. **(7)** If you like, you may top it up with more basil and serve it hot.

259. CHICKEN DITALINI

Total Time: 30 minutes | Prep Time: 10 minutes

Ingredients:

1 boneless, skinless chicken breast	Salt and pepper to taste
1 cup ditalini pasta	1 cup diced carrots
1 cup frozen peas	2 cups chicken broth
1/4 cup grated Parmesan cheese	

Directions:

(1) Add salt & pepper to the chicken breast. **(2)** Throw the chicken breast, ditalini pasta, carrots (chopped), peas (frozen), and chicken stock into the rice cooker. **(3)** Put the rice cooker cover on and simmer for 25 minutes . **(4)** Take the chicken breast out of the oven and shred it with two forks when the cooking cycle has finished. **(5)** Reintegrate the chicken shreds into the spaghetti sauce. **(6)** While stirring, melt the grated Parmesan and mix well. **(7)** Warm the dish before serving and top with more Parmesan cheese, if preferred.

260. CHICKEN ZITI

Total Time: 30 minutes | Prep Time: 10 minutes

Ingredients:

1 boneless, skinless chicken breast
1 cup ziti pasta
1/2 cup shredded mozzarella cheese
Salt and pepper to taste
1 cup marinara sauce
1/4 cup chopped fresh parsley

Directions:

(1) Add salt & pepper to the chicken breast. *(2)* In a rice cooker, combine the chicken breast, ziti, and marinara sauce. *(3)* Pour in just enough water to submerge the items. *(4)* Put the rice cooker cover on and simmer for 25 minutes . *(5)* Take the chicken breast out of the oven and shred it with two forks when the cooking cycle has finished. *(6)* Reintegrate the chicken shreds into the spaghetti sauce. *(7)* Toss in some shredded mozzarella and set aside for a minute to melt. *(8)* If preferred, serve hot with chopped fresh parsley as a garnish.

261. CHEESE FONDUE

Total Time: 25 minutes | Prep Time: 10 minutes

Ingredients:

1 cup shredded Gruyere cheese
1 clove garlic, minced
1 tablespoon cornstarch
1/4 teaspoon ground nutmeg
1 cup shredded Emmental cheese
1 cup dry white wine
1 tablespoon lemon juice
Assorted dippers (bread cubes, apple slices, steamed vegetables)

Directions:

(1) Put the minced garlic and shredded cheese into the rice cooker. *(2)* Add the cornstarch and white wine and whisk until combined in a separate bowl. *(3)* Combine the wine mixture with the cheese in the rice cooker. *(4)* Once combined, add the nutmeg and lemon juice and mix. *(5)* After adding the cheese, cover the rice cooker and simmer on "keep warm" for around 15 minutes , stirring every so often, until the cheese is melted and completely smooth. *(6)* Top with a variety of dippers and serve right away.

262. CHANA MASALA

Total Time: 30 minutes | Prep Time: 10 minutes

Ingredients:

1 can chickpeas, drained
2 cloves garlic, minced
1 can diced tomatoes
1 teaspoon ground cumin
1/2 teaspoon turmeric
1 onion, finely chopped
1 tablespoon olive oil
1 tablespoon tomato paste
1 teaspoon ground coriander
1/4 teaspoon cayenne pepper (adjust to taste)
Salt and pepper to taste
Chopped fresh cilantro for garnish

Directions:

(1) While the rice is cooking, soften the garlic and onion in olive oil. *(2)* Incorporate the chickpeas, tomato paste, seasonings, and chopped tomatoes. Mix thoroughly. *(3)* After 15 minutes of cooking on the "cook" setting, cover the rice cooker and remove the lid. *(4)* At this point, taste it to see if you need more

salt or pepper. **(5)** Warm the dish and top it with chopped cilantro.

263.   DEVILED EGGS

Total Time: 20 minutes | Prep Time: 10 minutes

Ingredients:

6 large eggs	3 tablespoons mayonnaise
1 teaspoon Dijon mustard	1/2 teaspoon white vinegar
Salt and pepper to taste	Paprika for garnish

Directions:

(1) Before adding water to the rice cooker, make sure the eggs are covered with water. **(2)** Toss the rice into the rice cooker and let it cook for 10 minutes on the "cook" setting. **(3)** After the eggs are done, take them out of the pan and let them cool in cold water. **(4)** Before halving the eggs, remove their shells. Put the yolks in a basin after removing them. **(5)** Blend the egg yolks with the mayonnaise, mustard, vinegar, salt, and pepper until they are completely smooth. **(6)** To re-use the egg whites, spoon or pipe the yolk mixture into them. **(7)** As a finishing touch, sprinkle with paprika.

264.   CHICKEN GYRO

Total Time: 30 minutes | Prep Time: 15 minutes

Ingredients:

1 pound boneless, skinless chicken breasts	2 tablespoons olive oil
2 cloves garlic, minced	1 teaspoon dried oregano
1/2 teaspoon dried thyme	Salt and pepper to taste
4 pita bread rounds	Tzatziki sauce, lettuce, tomato, onion for serving

Directions:

(1) Garlic, sautéed in olive oil until aromatic, should be added to the rice cooker. **(2)** Slice the chicken and toss it with the oregano, thyme, salt, and pepper. Brown and cook the chicken until done. **(3)** Pita bread rounds may be warmed in a rice cooker for a short period of time. **(4)** Assemble by stuffing each pita round with cooked chicken, lettuce, tomato, and onion. **(5)** Glace on some tzatziki sauce. **(6)** Quickly prepare and serve.

265.   TERIYAKI CHICKEN

Total Time: 25 minutes | Prep Time: 10 minutes

Ingredients:

1 lb boneless, skinless chicken breasts	½ cup teriyaki sauce
2 tablespoons soy sauce	1 tablespoon honey
1 teaspoon minced garlic	1 teaspoon grated ginger
1 tablespoon vegetable oil	2 cups cooked white rice
Sesame seeds & sliced	green onions for garnish

Directions:

(1) Combine teriyaki sauce, soy sauce, honey, ginger, and garlic in a small bowl. **(2)** Utilize the "Sauté" feature on the rice cooker insert to heat the vegetable oil. **(3)** Brown the chicken pieces by adding them to the pan. **(4)** After you combine the teriyaki sauce and the chicken, toss to coat. **(5)** After adding the chicken, cover the rice cooker and simmer it for 10 to 15 minutes on the "Cook" setting or until done. *(6)* Top cooked rice with teriyaki chicken, then top with sesame seeds and green onion slices.

266.   CHICKEN CASARECCE

Total Time: 30 minutes | Prep Time: 15 minutes

Ingredients:	
1 lb casarecce pasta	1 lb boneless, skinless chicken thighs
1 tablespoon olive oil	1 cup chopped onion
1 cup sliced mushrooms	1 cup marinara sauce
½ cup chicken broth	2 cloves garlic, minced
Salt and pepper to taste	

Directions:

(1) Use the "Steam" setting on the rice cooker to cook the pasta as directed on the box. Rinse and reserve. *(2)* Using the "Sauté" feature, heat up some olive oil in the rice cooker insert. *(3)* Brown the chicken strips by adding them to the pan. *(4)* When the mushrooms & onions begin to soften, add them to the pan. *(5)* Blend in the chicken stock, garlic, salt, and pepper with the marinara sauce. *(6)* After adding the chicken & sauce to the rice cooker, cover and cook on the "Cook" setting for 10 to 15 minutes , or until the chicken is done and the sauce is hot. *(7)* Over-cooked spaghetti, spoon the chicken carcass.

267.   SHRIMP SATAY

Total Time: 20 minutes | Prep Time: 10 minutes

Ingredients:	
1 lb large shrimp, peeled and deveined	½ cup coconut milk
2 tablespoons peanut butter	1 tablespoon soy sauce
1 tablespoon lime juice	1 teaspoon minced garlic
1 teaspoon grated ginger	Bamboo skewers soaked in water

Directions:

(1) In a small bowl, mix together the satay sauce ingredients: peanut butter, coconut milk, soy sauce, lime juice, ginger, and garlic. *(2)* Put the moistened bamboo skewers on top of the shrimp. *(3)* Toss the skewers with the satay sauce and set them in the rice cooker insert. *(4)* For around seven to ten minutes , or until the shrimp become pink and are cooked through, put the rice cooker on the "Cook" setting with the lid closed. *(5)* Warm up some more sauce and serve the shrimp satay hot.

268.   HERB ROASTED CHICKEN

Total Time: 30 minutes | Prep Time: 10 minutes

Ingredients:	
1 whole chicken, about 3-4 lbs	2 tablespoons olive oil
2 tablespoons	1 teaspoon garlic
chopped fresh herbs	powder
1 teaspoon onion powder	Salt and pepper to taste

Directions:

(1) Combine olive oil, minced herbs, onion & garlic seasonings, salt & pepper to coat the chicken. **(2)** Lay the chicken breast side down in the rice cooker insert. **(3)** Once the chicken is half-done and browned, cover the rice cooker and put it on the "Cook" setting for 25 to 30 minutes . **(4)** Carve the chicken after it has rested for a few minutes. **(5)** Arrange your preferred accompaniments beside the herb-roasted chicken.

269. CHICKEN SHAWARMA

Total Time: 25 minutes | Prep Time: 15 minutes

Ingredients:

1 lb boneless, skinless chicken thighs	2 tablespoons olive oil
2 tablespoons shawarma seasoning	1 cup Greek yogurt
2 tablespoons lemon juice	2 cloves garlic, minced
Salt and pepper to taste	Pita bread, lettuce, tomatoes, and cucumbers for serving

Directions:

(1) Mix together the olive oil, shawarma spice, garlic, lemon juice, salt, & pepper in a bowl. After 10 minutes of marinating, add the chicken slices. **(2)** Use the "Sauté" mode to heat the rice cooker insert. **(3)** Brown and thoroughly cook the marinated chicken in a rice cooker. **(4)** Combine the Greek yogurt and a teaspoon of salt in a separate dish. **(5)** Gather some warm pita bread, some lettuce, some tomatoes, some cucumbers, and a dollop of Greek yogurt to go with the chicken shawarma.

THE END

THE END

Made in the USA
Monee, IL
06 December 2024

72670926R00059